MILTON,
CHALKWELL,
AND THE
CROWSTONE

MARION PEARCE

Ian Henry Publications

ISBN 0 86025 510 7

Published by Ian Henry Publications, Ltd.
20 Park Drive, Romford, Essex RM1 4LH
and printed by
Hobbs the Printers, Ltd.
Brunel Road, Totton, Hampshire SO40 3WX

INTRODUCING MILTON

This is the history of Milton, a name almost lost in the mists of time. It is the story of the founding of Southend and Westcliff, an area steeped in history. The name Milton has passed from the town's memory and sunk into oblivion, but there are still traces left in Southend. I hope this book will revive those traces. Here is the story of the growth and death of a town called Milton.

The town's name was derived from its position of being the middle settlement between Leigh and Southchurch. In the earliest records it is written as Middletun, Middletuna, Meletun and Mildentun before becoming Milton, a name by which the region was known by for nearly one thousand years.

It is interesting to note that possibly the first record of Southend appears in the accounts of the Manor of Milton in 1309 as a small area of five and half acres of land worth only two shilling and nine pence called 'Stratende". This could said to have been the origin of Southend, rather than the more common theory from later sources that modern Southend grew from the southern end of the Manor of Prittlewell.

Legend has it that Milton used to have its own church which was destroyed by floods and that the ruins of the church could be seen at low tide. On a stormy day it was said that the church bells could be heard, ringing in the distance. If the church existed (which has long been a matter of debate) Milton would have been a parish in her own right rather than part of the Parish of Prittlewell. Certainly there are records of large floods in the area in 1099 and 1327. The Anglo-Saxon Chronicles state that in 1099 a large flood decimated the whole country. It records:

"This year (1099) at Martinmas, the great sea-flood came up and did so much harm that no man remembered its like before, that was the same day of the new moon."

The 1327 flood caused forty acres of land to be reclaimed by the sea at Milton and could well be the flood referred to in the legend. Local people remember their parents telling them of sightings of a ruins of a building visible in the distance at low tide. Frequent glimpses of these remains in the sea have been seen right up to the last century.

Philip Benton, in his *History of Rochford Hundred* in 1866, stated that Milton stretched from Leigh Pottery (now the corner of Leigh Road at Chalkwell Park), through Chalkwell Hall, passing the Cricketers' Inn, the Waterworks, towards the Shore House, and northwards towards Milton Hall (now known as Nazareth House), and eastward nearly to Porters. All of which has been swallowed up by an insignificant part of the shoreline with a jetty and some oyster beds known as Southend and Westcliff.

Milton continued to be the principal name by which the area was known until 1869 when the Milton Estate became one of the first estates in the parish to be sold for housing. Until absorbed into Southend between 1860 and 1880 the region was known as the Hamlet of Milton, or more simply, Milton Hamlet, being: 'within one and half miles of that increasing fashionable bathing place Southend.'

The name 'The Hamlet' can still be seen in the naming of roads in the town e.g. Hamlet Road, Hamlet Court Road. Gradually the name of Milton and Milton Hamlet was lost as building contractors preferred to use the more marketable names of

'Westcliff on-Sea' and 'Southend-on-Sea'.

Milton, the origin of Southend and Westcliff, gradually faded from the town's memory, forgotten, just an echo left lingering in a few street names and the name of an electoral ward. In 1987 the area was made into the Milton Conservation area and the Milton Conservation Society was formed to protect its heritage. Perhaps it is now time to look back and remember the true source of the Borough of Southend, and Westcliff.

ESSEX

ROCHFORD
HUNDRED.

Manor of
Milton Hall in
Prittlewell.

HALF HUNDRED OF ROCHFORD.—MILDENTUNA is held by the Holy Trinity for a manor and ii. hides. Always viii. villeins. Then xiii. bordars, now xv. Always i. serf and ii. teams in the demesne, and vi. teams of the homagers. Wood for lx. swine, and viii. beasts and ii. horses and xxv. swine and cxxiv. sheep. It was then worth c. shillings, and is now worth viii. pounds.

An extract from the Little Domesday - Essex

SAXON AND NORMAN MILTON

England was, at the end of the 10th century, experiencing a period of relative calm under the guidance of King Edgar (957-975) after the turmoil of the decades of Viking Raids. Christianity flourished as monastic orders from Canterbury radiated out over the country to spread the word of Christ to the local populace.

In the year 959, the Manor of Milton was granted to the Monks of Christchurch, Canterbury.

The *extent* or land accounts of 1309 describe the event thus:
'In the reign of our Lord's Incarnation of 959, I, Angleward, Thegn of King Edgar give to the Monks there serving God, with the consent of My Lord King Edgar, a Township of my patrimony, named Meleton [Milton], free of all secular service and payment, except for the maintenance of bridges and fortresses.

Describing Milton as a 'township' indicates that there was already some form of settlement at Milton. The 'ton' in the name Milton is from the Old English *tun*, originally meaning 'enclosure' although the definition later come to be 'enclosure surrounding a dwelling' and later still to a 'homestead' or a 'village'. All settlements during this period were probably fortified to guard against attack from the Vikings.

Certainly, Essex in the late 10th century was particularly vulnerable to attack. The sea, which was a major trade route, was used by the Vikings as a highway to invade Britain. By the late 10th and early 11th centuries Danish raids were common again in Essex, the most famous being the Battle of Maldon in 991 and the Battle of Assandun in 1016, said to be fought at Ashington.

The ownership of Milton was confirmed in a Charter by Edward the Confessor (1042-66) in 1065, which stated:
'If anyone shall hereafter presume to deprive them of their lawful right, or shall consent to the same, let them forever be anathematised and damned with the traitor Judas.'

Britain at the time of the Norman Conquest in 1066 was mainly an agricultural country. She had recovered from earlier Viking wars and was now settled into a land of rural peace.

By the time of the Domesday Book in 1086 Milton had grown into a sizable farming community of approximately 240 acres. The land was worked by two villeins, who were men with a substantial landholding in the estate. The villein was obliged to perform a variety of services and pay a range of fines in return for his right to farm his land, graze his livestock on the common pasture, and collect hay from the common meadow. His daughter could not marry without his lord's consent and had to pay a fine called *merchet*, and upon his death a fine called *heriot* was imposed on his heirs. At Milton the villeins were assisted by one serf, and fifteen bordars. A bordar was one of the lowest ranks in the feudal system, allowed to cultivate a very small amount of land, barely enough to live on, and in return had to perform menial work for his lord either free or for a very small sum. The estate supported 80 beast, two horses, 25 swine and 126 sheep, with woods large enough for sixty swine to forage in. In 1086 the annual value of the estate was calculated at one hundred shillings. Although difficult to calculate, one shilling in the late 11th century was worth approximately £50 in 1978.

By the late 13th century the *compotus* or accounts of 1299 shows that the running of the Manor of Milton was left to the Serjeant, a man who in feudal society held a position midway between that of a yeoman and a knight. He was paid thirteen shillings and four pence per year plus a bushel of wheat weekly, except during the five weeks of autumn harvesting when together with other servants he was also fed 'at the Lords Table'. He was assisted by a *Messor,* a manorial officer who managed the collective use of the common fields, and supervised the harvesting. The *Messor* was paid three shillings, and a stacker at harvesting was paid two shillings. There was also an Oxherd, Cowherd, and Shepherd who were paid a lamb and fleece each yearly, a Lamb Watcher, four Ploughmen, a Carter and three Grooms who were each paid in rye, one Maid who was paid three shillings yearly and a half bushel of rye. The estate was valued in 1291 as being worth £18.7s.8d. per year.

In 1309 Milton had grown into a rural community of 380 acres 3 roods (a rood being a quarter of an acre). Of this, 211 acres were under cultivation, the remaining land, about one-third of the total, was unused for cultivation, but left fallow, which meant that it was still valuable meadow land for pasturing animals who would enrich the land with their waste. On the 211 acres that was cultivated were grown a variety of crops, the majority being oat and wheat with twenty two acres of rye and only seven acres used for the growing of beans, peas and vetches (a plant of the pea family). There was also a valuable fifteen acres of wood. Most of the farming income came from the sale of corn, which raised £23.0s.9d. per year. Sheep provided an income with the sale of stock valued at £7.17s.1d. per year and the sale of wool £34.18s.1d. Sheep milk was made into cheese which was one of the staples of the peasants' diet, brought an income of £2.15s.4d. yearly. Milton also had prospering mussel beds in the estuary and the fishing of them brought the estate an income of £2 per year.

FARMING LANDS IN MILTON 1309

Field called Pirifeld	97 acres	worth £2.8s.6d. per year
Field called Menedfeld	23 acres	worth £2.3s.0d. per year
Field called Kyngestonesfeld	57 acres	worth £1.18s.4d per year
Field called Halvehide	43 acres, 3 roods	worth £2.3s.9d. per year
Field called Abramslond	13 acres	worth 6s.5d. per year
Field called West Mille	5 acres	worth 2s.6d. per year
Field called Northfield	116 acres	worth £4.16s.8d. per year
Field called Goselond	20 acres	worth 10s.0d. per year
Place called Suthmede	5.5 acres	worth 2s.9d. per year
Total acreage in 1309	380 acres, 3 roods.	
Total Value in 1309		£13. 12s.0d.

It is interesting to note that is a 'Suthmede', a place of five and a half acres worth two shillings and nine pence, the first mention of Southend? If so, Southend originated as the south end of Milton rather than Prittlewell.

By 1309 Milton appears to have been a self contained community, even having its own gallows, court, hall and mill.

During this period Milton was run by a very active prior, Prior Henry of Eastry in Kent, the Prior of the Monastery of the Monks of Christchurch. The Prior acted as Lord of the Manor and had extensive privileges and franchises, including the right to hold court and oversee the gallows, which latter was in a field near the sea. At Milton Prior Henry instigated an extensive building programme.

NEW BUILDINGS IN MILTON 1284-1321

1293 New Dove House and Waggon Shed	£1.10s.0d
1299 New Mill	£15.5s.10d.
1305 New Hall	£30.11s.0d.
1308 New Sheepcote	£1.2s.0d.
1310 New Outhouse and Dairy	£3.10s.3d.

In 1327 Milton was hit by a great natural disaster, a flood, over forty acres of land was reclaimed by the sea. Prior Henry at the Monastery assessed the considerable damage as: forty acres of land worth twelve pence per acre annually, marsh on which one hundred and twenty sheep could be reared worth four pounds per year. Also submerged was a water mill from which monastery obtained ten quarters of mixtil, a mixture of wheat and rye which was made into bread for the local peasants. This was the first reference to what was later known as Hamlet Mill.

This was a heavy blow to the community, forty acres of good farming land, a mill, and a substantial amount of marsh land capable of supporting sheep was a loss which would take the settlement a long while to recover from. The arable land having a yearly value two pounds, the sheep a value of four pounds annually and the mill an annual value of one pound, made the total loss worth seven pounds per year. A sizeable loss as the net profit from farming the whole estate in 1309 was only £24.18.4¾d. The flood was so large and widespread that it is likely that the coastline would have been permanently altered, things would never look the same again.

It could be the flood in 1327 that was the start of the legend of the Lost Church of Milton. It was said that a church had been lost to the sea and at low tide the ruins of a church could be seen which was the lost church of Milton. It was said that on stormy days, when the sea was rough, the church bells could be heard, ringing in the distance.

MILTON ACCOUNTS FOR THE YEAR 1298/9

	£. s. d.	£. s. d.
LORD OF THE MANOR'S INCOME		
Rent of assize	£5.10.9	
Perquisites of Court	£1.13.5	
		£7.4s.2d

LORD OF THE MANOR'S EXPENDITURE		
Protecting the liberty	£0.7.8	
Holding courts and Steward's fee	£1.2.7	
		£1.10s.3d

NET INCOME DIRECTLY DUE THE LORD OF THE MANOR
£5.13s.11d.

FARMING INCOME

Sale of Customary Services	£3.6.2¾	
Profits of Herbage	£2.0.8	
Rent of Mussel Laying	£2.0.0	
Sale of Corn	£2.3.09¾	
Sale of Stock	£7.17.1	
Sale of Wool	£4.18.1	
Profits of Dairy	£2.15.4	
		£45.18s.2½d

FARMING EXPENDITURE		
Expenses of Management, Audit, Wages, and Harvest Allowance	£10.1.3¼	
Purchase of Corn and Stock	£6.9.4¾	
Capital Expenditure on Buildings	£1.8.1	
Maintenance of buildings	£1.17.11½	
Other expenses	£1.3.1¼	
		£20.19s.9¾d.

Net profit from farming		£24.19s.9¾d.

PRIOR HENRY OF EASTRY

Henry of Eastry was Prior of the Monks of Christ Church, Canterbury, from 1285 to 1331, the longest serving Prior of Canterbury. He was in effect 'Lord of the Manor' of Milton. In 1893, a collection of over 400 of his letters were discovered in a stables in the Precincts of Canterbury Cathedral. These were called the *Eastry Correspondence* and has enabled historians to compile a picture of the mediæval life of this remarkable man. I am also indebted to Mr J R C Wright for his previously unpublished work on Henry of Eastry. It is interesting to delve a little further into the life and times of this important man.

An early 15th century chronicle describes him as:
'from that outstanding man, H de Eastry, who ruled the said church most vigorously for 47 years ... and left it free (of debt)'.

As Prior he was head of the centralised estate administration of all the vast lands belonging to Christ Church and it was his responsibility to manage the Manor of Milton. He was independent from his direct superior, the Archbishop of Canterbury.

Eastry became a monk as a young man and the 15th century chronicles describe how he began to grow in virtue 'and through zealous attention at the cloister acquired fluency in the Scriptures with an eager heart'. His achievements as Prior followed: his additions to the monastery's buildings, lands and revenues, his gifts of ornaments, vestments and books.

Professor D Knowles in his book *The Religious Orders in England* gives a portrait of Eastry:
'Henry of Eastry's priorate was ... one of the most peaceful Christ Church has known ... his thoughts worked the round of market prices, of stones of cheese, of bushels per acre, of the income from agistry, of the quality of the season's clip of wool. Stiff, dry and masterful, a great high farmer and superbly able man of business, he passes before us as he rides about the manors of sits at the chequer'.

When Henry of Eastry was elected as a Prior in 1285, at the age of 35, Christ Church was in debt. £5,000 was owed, the equivalent of two years gross revenue. It was by his sound direction that by the time of his death these large deficits were cleared.

He was a superb manager and at a time when the chief form of income in the country was agriculture, and was an excellent farmer. Under the mediæval system of the monastic estates, farming was run on a centralised system of management with the Prior at the head. As Prior, Henry of Eastry would be responsible for all the immense estates of Christ Church, Canterbury, including Milton. After touring his estates he would make his proposals for the management of the lands which he would then delegate to his senior monks, monk-wardens and bailiffs who between them ran the various estates. The senior monks ran the priory exchequer and audited the accounts. The monk wardens had responsibility for one of each of the four custodies: East Kent;

A document issued by Prior Henry (*by permission of the Dean & Chapter of Canterbury*)

An enlargement of Prior Henry's seal *(by permission of the Dean & Chapter of Canterbury)*

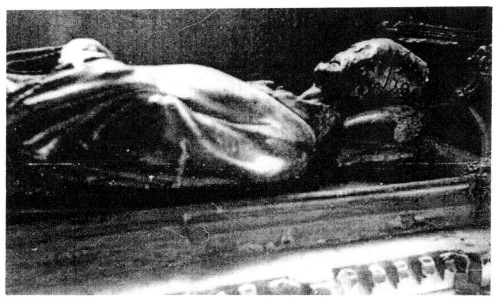

Prior Henry's tomb in Canterbury Cathedral *(by permission of the Dean & Chapter of Canterbury)*

the Weald and Romney Marsh; Essex; and the Thames Valley counties of Surrey, Buckinghamshire, and Oxfordshire. He appointed the bailiffs, and twice a year at Easter-tide and September would tour his custodies with a lay clerk giving instruction for the general running of the estate. Everything was recorded in great detail, even down to allowances set aside to pay the 'women who prepared the guts for the sausage skins.'

As Prior, Henry of Eastry was also responsible for the administration of justice in all lands belonging to Christ Church. The importance the Prior attached to this can be seen by Eastry's own library of 80 volumes, of which 29 were about Canon Law and 10 Civil Law. In 1321 Eastry recorded the conclusion of 21 lawsuits on terms favourable to Christ Church at a cost of £4,500. This was about a quarter of the total spent by Christ Church on taxes, lawsuits, on the various manors and monasteries owned by them excluding household expenses, which was valued at £18,000 for that year.

An example of his judgement can be found in the case of villagers of Bocking in Essex. The villagers were suffering from the discrimination of an overzealous steward, John Le Doo. They appealed to Prior Henry that excessive charges had been made against them saying:

'Against all reason and against the Great Charter that Holy Church ought to Maintain.'

The tenants complained that their case at court had been held illegally early, and then they had been fined for non-attendance. They also accused the steward of forcing them to mow the lord's meadow when they were exempt from that task. The Prior considered there requests and, after consulting his Council on the matter replied:

'the deed had not been do none by him nor by his wish and that in future he would not suffer such evil to be done to any tenant of the village but that they should be maintained in their customs in all matters'.

Another insight into the character of Prior Henry in this turbulent period of English history can be gained from his handling of a fierce dispute which occurred between the City of Canterbury and the monks in the monastery there in 1327, the same year in which the flood decimated Milton. The dispute was over taxes due to pay for Edward II's Scottish campaign. The citizens of Canterbury claimed that £200 of rents and 500 acres, belonging to Christ Church within the City of Canterbury were not exempt from taxation and they wanted the monastery to pay their share. They threatened to attack the monastery, to seize carts bringing it supplies, to arrest all monks leaving its gates, to refuse to trade with it, to prevent anyone from living in its property in the City, to use dues payable to Christ Church for the citizens of Canterbury, to prevent any pilgrim approaching unless he had sworn that he would make no offering to St Thomas, to take a gold ring for each citizen from the shrine, and to dig a ditch round the whole area. The Archbishop of Canterbury appealed to the citizens of the city, reminding them of the profit that St Thomas bought them and advised them to consult the Holy Spirit.

Prior Henry remained firm, claiming that he was unable and quite unwilling to weaken or burden the foundation and free state of the Church of Christ without the consent of its patron and founder. If the citizens persisted the monastery would rely on the King, whose ancestors made them free. Finally Prior Henry won, and the citizens of Canterbury relinquished their claims.

This was the era of great pilgrimages to see relics of saints. A huge and rich industry sprung up and vast wealth was created for the religious houses of the period. One of the most popular of these was a pilgrimage to visit the remains of St Thomas. Thomas à Becket (1118-70), Archbishop of Canterbury, was murdered by four of Henry II's barons in the Cathedral. This event shocked Christendom and in 1173 he was canonized as St Thomas of Canterbury. Many miracles were reported at his tomb in the cathedral, 703 alone within the next ten years. Canterbury Cathedral was soon doing a roaring trade in pilgrims visiting St Thomas's relics. They would make a tour of the Cathedral, including the saint's shrine; the Corona where a part of his skull was exposed in a silver reliquary; the place of martyrdom in the north-west transept; the sword point which slew the martyr, which was preserved in a special case; a piece of the saint's brain and his gold ring. The average income to the Cathedral from the relics of St Thomas was between £200 and £500, reaching a peak in 1320. Eastry himself often evoked 'the love of St Thomas' in his correspondence

It is interesting to note that Thomas, when Archbishop of Canterbury, placed great importance in Prittlewell Priory and the township of Milton. He took them under his wing and stated in his charter:

'The solicitude of the office we have taken upon us warns us to be watchful to carefully see to the peace and quietness of the servants of God. Therefore, we have under God our care the monastery of the Blessed Mary of Pritewell [Prittlewell] with its chapels of Sutton and Eastwood and with the tithings of the township of Middleton [Milton] and all the parochial rights of the said township.'

Milton at this time was still classified as a 'township', a term denoting a settlement. A township in mediæval documents could mean any settlement, large or small, and was not the counterpart of a modern town.

There were many great expenses to be met by the monastery. In 1321 £1,342.13s.4d. were paid in subsidies for the Holy Land and Curia, and in papal procurations; £4,611.8s. was sent to the royal household in 'taxes, gift, and exactions'; and £274.18s. was spent on defence by sea and land against the enemy, the French. These items accounted for about one third of expenditure on improvements to the estates and monastery, and in lawsuits and taxes. The King also has the right to appoint one or two 'pensioners' who live off the monastery. In 1318 Eastry refused to accept one of the pensioners, appealing to the King:

'We are so oppressed with sojourners and exhibitions and heavy fees and pensions and numerous aids and demands ... therefore Sire we pray you..... that for God's sake and for the love of St Thomas you will spare us.'

11

Prior Henry of Eastry built many impressive additions to Canterbury Cathedral. In 1304 a stone screen was built which encircles the choir, running from the stalls to the High Altar. The screen is a fine example of decorative work. In the same year the Chapter House was repaired with two new gabled walls in similar style to the choir screen. The work that Prior Henry had carried out on the Chapter House is described by Canon Ingram Hill in his book *Canterbury Cathedral*:

The largest of its kind in England, it was rebuilt by Prior Eastry in 1304, its Romanesque predecessor most likely being a rectangle of modest proportions like other Norman Chapter Houses which survive unaltered as at Bristol and Gloucester.'

He kept the rectangular shape but created a huge hall, nearly a hundred feet in length, with a noble doorway, a double stone seat for the monks running the round the sides with an arcade behind, and at the east end a throne-like seat for the prior.

The additions to both the choir and the Chapter House cost £839.7s.8d. and they can still be seen in Canterbury Cathedral, lasting monuments of Prior Henry's achievements.

New vestments and altar piece and other ornaments to the cathedral were also bought by Henry at a cost of £147.14s. The new vestments consisted of a chasuble, which was a sleeveless cloak varying in colour according to the season; a cope, which was a sleeveless cloak worn on festive occasions; a tunic; and a dalmatic, which was a tunic worn at High Mass under a chasuble. Each of these were made of red samite, a mediæval silk fabric, embroidered with the arms of the King of England. Another set of vestments was of Indian samite, decorated with stars and crescents and yet a third was crafted from Turkish samite. The spectacle at mass must indeed have been of 'jewelled brightness'.

£147.14s. was spent on the shrine of St Thomas, which had a new gold crest and was decorated with gold, silver, and precious stones. Among the building work undertaken by the prior was eight new bells for the cathedral at a cost of £236.14s. As a memorial, one of the bells still rung today in the Cathedral is named 'Bell Harry'.

Prior Eastry interests were also in theological matters. In surviving documents there are references to the great religious debates of the day; the advent of Antichrist, the four ways in which Antichrist deceives the people, and the followers of Antichrist, the duration of the time of persecution and the death of Antichrist, the first beginnings from which sin arose, a morbid delight in sin, the effect of hearing mass by day, the constitutions of Henry II for which the blessèd Thomas was martyred, conscience, and even the number of a legion and the size of Noah's Ark.

Prior Henry died while celebrating Mass in Canterbury Cathedral aged 92. To be aged 92, when during this period the average monk died aged 50.2 years would have enabled Eastry to enjoy exceptional prestige. He was buried in Canterbury Cathedral and is the only tomb of a prior in the cathedral, a mark of the great respect in which he was held. His effigy shows him as he was remembered, in his mitre and vestments. The tomb cost the Prior £21.3s.4d. and is a fitting memorial to this remarkable man.

MEDIÆVAL MILTON

In the 14th century Milton suffered with the rest of the country a disaster which could only be compared in modern terms to the aftermath of a nuclear explosion - the Black Death. Nearly a third of the population of the country died in a short time. The Black Death was also frightening for, as well as being lethal to people, livestock died as a result of there being not enough people left alive to care for them. Although no records exist in Milton of human casualties surviving, there is a record of relatively large loss of cattle to the community, seven oxen, eleven cows with their calves, and sixty sheep having died.

The Black Death radically altered the balance of the population to the land. Suddenly the ordinary farming folk were in high demand to work the land. The peasants seized the opportunity to demand better rights and conditions for themselves, which erupted as the Peasants' Revolt led by Wat Tyler.

In 1381 Milton became involved in the rebellion. The villagers stormed Milton Hall in protest at the poor wages and conditions and burned the manorial records, but their attempt at freedom proved fruitless and they were forced to pay large fines.

During the greater part of the 14th century England was at war with her historic enemy, France. Tensions rose to such a point that invasion seemed imminent and, in 1385, the government ordered all available men to arm themselves to fight the French. The south-eastern coast was considered particularly vulnerable and beacons were to be erected where there was a serious danger from the enemy to warn people of the peril of attack. Milton erected its beacon where Cliff Town Parade now stands. The beacon was still standing on 23rd March, 1667, as a bill was presented to Prittlewell parishioners for £5.15s.0d. for the beacon watch, consisting of firing, pitch and tar. Payment was refused and the dispute was finally settled by the Treasurer of Essex paying the account.

By the 14th century Milton stretched from Chalkwell Park in the west to the border of Prittlewell in the east. In 1580 Chalkwell Hall was held in the Manor of Milton for an annual rent of twenty-three shillings and three pence.

When King Henry VIII (1509-47) ordered the dissolution of the monasteries the entire estates of Milton passed from the monks of Christchurch, Canterbury, to the hands of one of Henry's favourites, Sir Richard Rich, on 20th March, 1539. The priory of Christchurch was dissolved, its revenues reverting to the Crown. The dissolution was completed on the 20th January, 1545, when Henry granted the Manors of Middleton (Milton), Southchurch, Lawling, and Styfted to Sir Richard Rich.

Sir Richard Rich was a powerful man. In 1533 he was appointed Solicitor-General and two years later became Chirographer (a form of legal secretary) of the King's Bench. He became Speaker of the House of Commons in 1537 and in 1548 was made Lord Chancellor and the 1st Baron Rich. He kept the chancellorship for only three years as, in 1553, he unwisely proclaimed Lady Jane Grey as Queen.

After seeing the error of his ways he changed sides to support the reigning queen, Mary, and in doing so persecuted many Protestants. The Rich family owned a lot of land locally, residing at Rochford Hall.

In the 16th century the country was in turmoil, caught between two religions, Catholicism and Protestantism. Henry VIII had started the wheels of change turning when he divorced his first wife, Catherine of Aragon, against the Pope's wishes, to marry Anne Boleyn. After many years of marriage Catherine had only produced a female child, the future Queen Mary, and he hoped that Anne would give birth to a male son and heir to the throne. He did not think that the country would accept a female sovereign of England, who would be the first to rule in her own right since Empress Matilda had attempted to take the throne four hundred years before. The Pope refused to grant him a divorce and Henry broke with Rome, declaring himself head of the Church of England. Edward VI (1547-53), son of Henry VIII and Jane Seymour, accelerated the Reformation, and England became a Protestant country. Thus the religion of the country changed in a fairly short time from the old Catholicism to the new Protestantism. People were caught in the middle, to be in the wrong religion meant being charged with heresy and, if found guilty, sentenced to be burnt at the stake.

It was at this period that Milton became a refuge for those escaping persecution. Milton at this time still had areas of marsh and was relatively inaccessible to the rest of the country. Milton also had a reasonable sized port where passage could be bought for France or the Low Countries and freedom, making it an ideal escape route.

One of the first martyrs of the reformation, John Frith, was arrested at Milton Shore in 1534, charged with heresy. He was studying for the Roman Catholic priesthood at what is now known as Christchurch, Cambridge. While there he renounced the Catholic faith for the teachings of Martin Luther, Protestantism. He was imprisoned but escaped, fleeing to Milton where he was later arrested while trying to fly to the continent. Accused of heresy he was brought before Sir Thomas Cromwell and, after being cross-examined by Sir Thomas Cranmer, was found guilty and sentenced to be burnt at the stake at Smithfield with another dissenter. John Frith died slowly, in acute agony, it taking two hours for the flames to kill him, because he was actually burnt, rather than asphyxiated.

When Mary came to the throne she tried to drag the country back to Catholicism; the cause of much rebellion throughout her reign, earning her the name of 'Bloody Mary' because of the many executions of people she ordered.

In her turbulent reign another rebel, Edwin Sandys, Vice-Chancellor of Cambridge University, was more fortunate. In 1553, after the death of Edward VI, Dr Sandys proclaimed Lady Jane Grey queen instead of Mary. It proved to be a bad choice. Imprisoned in the Tower of London, he escaped and fled to the house of his step-father at Woodham Ferrers, but after two hours he had to flee again to Milton Shore, where he hid in the house of a mariner named James Mower. Mower, who after eight years of marriage was childless, treated Dr Sandys with kindness. On leaving Dr Sandys prophesied, 'Be of good comfort, ere one year be past, God will give you a son'. Legend has it that Mower's wife gave birth to a son one year later.

Before escaping to Flanders Dr Sandys gave a sermon to 40-50 eager seamen who had gathered to hear him preach. He was a gifted orator and all the men assembled vowed to give their lives to protect him. With their help he escaped in the nick of time, the Queen's men in hot pursuit. He stayed in Flanders until the death of Queen Mary, then returning home. He later achieved the post of Archbishop of York. Dr Sandys' story was told by John Foxe in his *The Book of Martyrs*.

When Elizabeth ascended the throne after the death of Mary, she brought yet another change of religion, turning the country back to Protestantism.

In Elizabeth's reign a Catholic named Tyrrell tried to escape to Dunkirk or Bruges from Milton Shore. Unfortunately, stormy weather delayed his departure, the seas being too rough for his voyage. While waiting he is said to have composed the following poem:

Lyke as a Merchawnt, which on surginge seas
In beaten barcke hathe fellt the grevous rage
Of Aolus blasts, tyll Neptune for hys eas
Bye princelye power thear cholars did assage
    Even soe my muse

Doth seem by fortunes cruell spyte
To feel her cupp so myxt wth bytter galle
As noe conceapt coulld make her to delyght
Untyll she chawnst in scholoshypp to fall
    With you, my ffrend

Whom myghtye Jove hathe sent me for relefe,
When heavye cares woolld seek for to oppres
My pensyff mynd and slylye as a theffe
Holld me captyve styll in sore dystres.

Capturing his impatience and frustrations in verse perhaps took too much time writing as Tyrrell was arrested at Milton Shore and taken to Fleet Prison, London. He was later released and fled to Amsterdam in 1587.

Whether Milton was a separate parish is open to debate. Legend has it that the parish church was submerged by floods. The ruins of a building could be seen at low tide until about 1840. Certainly in the 17th century the villagers thought so. They refused to contribute to the road repairs on the grounds that Milton was a separate parish, not part of Prittlewell. In 1631 a Milton resident called Richard Keene refused to supply either a cart, team of horses or workmen for road repairs, and in 1631 so did George Malle of Porters Farm.

The dispute between Milton and Prittlewell continued for quite a few years. In 1611 the bridge over Prittle Brook in North Street, Prittlewell was in need of repairs and the parish was ordered to provide funds to repair it. The villagers refused responsibility. In 1616 they again refused saying that 'for who should make it we know not.' The dispute continued until 1678 when a parish vestry meeting was held to decide the matter. They ruled against Milton, who then had to contribute to bridge repairs. In 1813 the Kings Bench division made Milton a separate parish for the maintaining of highways. Milton had its own surveyor from 1697, an overseer from 1707 and a village constable from 1720.

It was in the mediæval period that Milton was at its zenith. It was then a thriving town, with a port and a self-contained community.

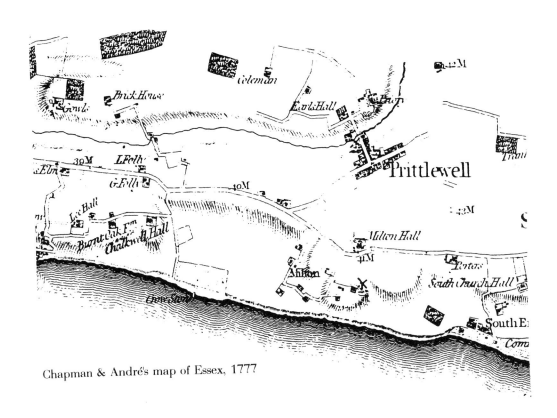

Chapman & Andrés map of Essex, 1777

HAMLET MILL

Records show that the earliest mill in Milton was a water mill situated beside the sea. In a memorandum of 1327 stating the flood damage of that year the water mill was said to produce ten quarters of mixtil. The mill was swept away and completely destroyed in the flood of that year.

In 1309 this early mill was let at a rent of twelve quarters of mixtil at about four shillings per quarter making a total rent of forty-eight shillings a year.

The Prior of the Monks of Christchurch Canterbury, Prior Henry of Eastry, built a replacement windmill of the post design as part of a large modernisation programme in 1299. This was one of the first post windmills built in Britain. The post mill was of a revolutionary new design. It is a type of mill built on a central post of wood standing on four wooden legs. The mill itself was pivoted on the top of the post, this enabled the mill to be pushed around so that the sails faced the prevailing wind. Thus the mill could be used in all weathers, whatever the direction of the wind, extending the working period of the building. This was a very early type of mill of wooden construction.

The cost was itemised as follows:
For carpentry work on the new mill and for its erection, by agreement
$£5.0s.0d.$
For carting the said mill from Bocking to Hebregg and for the further journey by water to Middleton [Milton] $£1.15s.10d.$
For iron and for the making of divers iron fittings $18s.7½d.$
For nails bought for the same purpose $3s.0d.$
And for grease $1s.1½d.$
For ramming around the mill post $2s.10d.$
For enlarging the mill mound by agreement $8s.2d.$
For the purchase of 2 mill stones and for the loading and carriage of these from Sandwich to Middleton (Milton) $£5.11s.4d.$
For 60 ells (45 ins per ell) of canvas bought for the sails at 5d the ell
$£1.5s.0d.$
TOTAL COST $£15.5s.10d.$

Thus the total cost of the mill in 1299 was fifteen pounds five shillings and ten pence: a very expensive building which shows the importance the mill had in the community, as in 1299 the serjeant who ran the whole Manor of Milton was only paid thirteen shillings and four pence a year.

Hamlet Mill was to play an important part in the upheavals that accompanied the late 14th and early 15th century England: a period of turmoil. Richard II was an unpopular monarch and Henry of Lancaster was challenging his right to rule. The country was seething with discontent. In May, 1399, Richard left England to quell a

Particulars

AND

CONDITIONS OF SALE,

OF VERY VALUABLE

WIND CORN-MILLS

LANDS,

AND

GENTEEL RESIDENCES,

(WITH POSSESSION AT MICHAELMAS NEXT,)

THE PROPERTY OF MR. J. D. KEMP,

DECEASED,

SITUATE AT PRITTLEWELL, IN ESSEX;

WHICH WILL BE

SOLD BY AUCTION,

BY CHALK AND MEGGY,

ON THURSDAY, MAY 23, 1811,

BY ORDER OF THE EXECUTORS,

AT THE NEW SHIP INN, ROCHFORD, ESSEX,

AT THREE O'CLOCK IN THE AFTERNOON.

———

₊ Particulars and Conditions of Sale may be had of Mr. Bathurst, Solicitor, Rochford; also at the Inns in the Neighbourhood; at the Auction Mart, London; and of the Auctioneers, Chelmsford.

PARTICULARS.

LOT I.

A nearly new - built POST WINDMILL, adjoining the Town of Prittlewell, constructed upon the best Principles, chiefly built with Oak, the Timbers of large Dimensions, and embracing every Advantage from Extent, having Sails thirty-six Feet long, standing remarkably well for Wind, capable of grinding twenty Loads per Week; with Brick Round-House, containing two Floors, independent of which the Mill has three Floors, carrying two Pair of capital French Stones, Flour and Clearing-off Machines; forming, from the State in which the Mill now stands, (being equal in every Respect to new,) a most advantageous Purchase to those who want Business, in a Situation surrounded by Lands producing the finest Wheats in this Kingdom. The Mill stands upon Four Acres, or thereabouts, of excellent Land, abutting upon the great Road, the Scite of which is extremely eligible for the Erection of a Dwelling-House.

☞ This Lot is Copyhold of the Manor of Milton Hall.

LOT II.

A very respectable and commodious FREEHOLD ESTATE, situate in a pleasant Part of the Town of Prittlewell, and a convenient Distance from Lot 1; comprising two genteel RESIDENCES, both including every requisite Accommodation for respectable Families. Annexed to this Lot is excellent Stabling, Chaise-house, Barn, Cow-house, Cart-sheds, Granary, Millwright's Shop, and other Conveniences; together with two Inclosures of rich Freehold Pasture and Arable Land, containing, with the Scite of the Buildings, &c. about Five Acres, be the same more or less.

This Lot will be sold subject to the Dwelling-House and Premises, also the Garden adjoining, and Half of the Garden opposite, as staked out at the East End, being occupied by Mrs. Kemp during her Life, at the yearly Rent of 17l. clear of all Taxes and Repairs. The above House, Yard, and Out-buildings, are divided from and unconnected with the other Premises. The Purchaser of this Lot will be required to execute a Lease to Mrs. Kemp, at her Expence, agreeably to the above Particulars.

LOT III.

A FREEHOLD POST WINDMILL, carrying, at present, one Pair of Stones, with Flour Machine, but capable of considerable Improvement, standing nearly opposite to Lot 1, and adjoining to Lot 2, upon about Half an Acre of rich Freehold Pasture Ground, abutting upon the great Road.

LOT IV.

An INCLOSURE of excellent FREEHOLD ARABLE LAND, nearly adjoining Lot 1, containing about Four Acres, be the same more or less.

Should the two first Lots be purchased by one Person, Part of the Purchase-Money may remain on Mortgage, if required.

The above Mills and Premises are situate only one Mile from South-End, from whence there is regular Water-Carriage to and from London; three Miles from Rochford, and are also surrounded by a rebellion in Ireland. Henry seized the opportunity to rebel and forced Richard to abdicate. A year later Richard died a prisoner in Pontefract Castle and a victorious Henry of Lancaster ascended the throne as Henry IV.

The general unrest affected Essex. In 1397, during the reign of Richard II, the king ordered the murder of one his uncles, Thomas of Woodstock, the Duke of Gloucester. Woodstock was ambushed at Stratford by John Holland, Duke of Exeter, and taken to Calais where he was strangled. His body was embalmed, encased in lead and taken by sea to Hadleigh Castle before being buried at Pleshy church, Essex.

Three years later, when Henry IV came to the throne, the Duke of Exeter, a half brother of the deposed Richard, was now on the wrong side. Henry was after him for treason. The Duke fled for his life to Milton Shore where he tried to board a ship to freedom. Unfortunately the weather was rough and high winds forced him to wait. He took refuge in Hamlet Mill while he waited for more favourable weather. It was here, while he was dining with John of Prittlewell, that the villagers of Milton found him. They besieged the mill and arrested the Duke of Exeter and took him to Pleshy Castle where he was severely tortured and then beheaded.

Hamlet Mill continued in the ownership of the Monks of Christchurch, Canterbury, until the dissolution of the monasteries by Henry VIII, when all lands owned by the church were seized by the Crown and redistributed to Henry's favourites at court. The mill passed with the rest of the estate to Lord Rich and later to Daniel Scratton.

In 1788 Mr. Scratton insured the timber built mill for £100. The insurance was increased in 1797 to £270 plus £80 for the machinery. On the 15th September, 1797, he placed an advertisement in the *Chelmsford Chronicle*:

TO LET

'A capital and old established windmill called Milton Hall Mill in the parish of Prittlewell in the county of Essex.'

The lease was taken by Edward Ellcock, a Miller and Mealman who, in 1799, insured the gears and stock in trade for £430. The mill now appears to be a valuable commodity.

Edward Ellcock added many improvements to the mill which now appears to be a prominent business with four acres of land surrounded by fields growing 'the best wheat in the kingdom' as the next the next description of the building shows, which appeared on May 23rd, 1811, when Hamlet Mill was the first lot of a sale of two mills: 'A nearly new built post windmill, adjoining the town of Prittlewell, constructed upon the best principles, chiefly built with oak, the timbers of large dimensions and embracing every advantage from extent, having sails 36 feet long, standing remarkably well for wind, capable of grinding 20 loads per week, with brick roundhouse, containing two floors independent of which the mill has three floors, carrying two pairs of capital French stones, flour and clearing-off machines forming from the state in which the mill now stands, (being equal in every respect to new) a most advantageous purchase to those who want business in a situation surrounded by lands producing the finest wheats in the kingdom. The mill stands upon four acres or thereabouts, of excellent land, abutting upon the Great Road, the site of which is extremely eligible for the erection of a dwelling house.'

An advertisement appeared again for the mill in the *Southend Standard* of July, 1880.

'A capital post windmill drawing to pairs of stones in good repair. Good residence with oven and bakehouse attached, five stables, coach house, piggeries and ten acres of arable and meadowland.'

The mill has been improved again since 1811 with the millhouse and bakery now built and the ground around it more than doubled from four acres to ten.

Hamlet Mill was still in good working order when it was sold with the estate by Daniel Scratton, Lord of the Manor, in 1869. Hamlet Mill and Mill House with land now totalling seventeen and a half acres formed one lot. It was then let on a yearly basis for £40 exclusive of rates and taxes, and was bought by Thomas Arnold for £1,000. It was only to be in operation for a few more years, for in the *Essex Weekly News* of 4th January, 1878, an advertisement appeared:

The materials of the Hamlet Mill pulled down which included 10,000 bricks, two tons of iron and many good sound oak beams.'

Hamlet Mill stood at the bottom of Park Road at the junction of Avenue Road opposite Park Road Methodist Church. The site is now occupied by a small parade of shops. Avenue Road was once known as Mill Lane and Love Lane and was a country byway leading from Milton to Prittlewell, hedged with primroses and violets.

Hamlet Mill, 1845 *(reproduced by courtesy of the Essex Record Office)*

MARITIME MILTON

Milton was a thriving port famous for its shipping and oysters in the 16th century. Britain in this period was a maritime nation, building its prosperity on its navy. The discovery of America had provided a wonderful opportunity for trade in a new continent and was the start of England's great Empire. The Essex ports played a large part in this growing commercial enterprise. In 1571 Milton had three ships of 50-100 tons and five ships under 50 tons docked in harbour. The shipping of the period from local ports were shown thus:

HOME PORT	BURDEN UNDER 50 TONS	50-100 TONS
Leigh	13	27
Milton	5	3
Barling	2	
Hullbridge	2	
Canewdon	2	
Total	24	30

Several Admiralty Courts were held at Milton Shore. In 1543 a precept was issued summoning jurors from South Benfleet to an Admiralty Court in Milton. The Bailiff and Constable were told under penalty of a fine of £5 to:
'admonish six, four, or two at least, honest men of that parish to appear before the Lord High Admiral of England, or his deputy, at the King's Court of the Admiralty, to be holden at Milton, in the said County of Essex.'

This note was signed by Richard Reed, Commissary. Richard Reed is likely to be the same man who valued the ship in John Scott's case.

On 28th June, 1539, John Scott, a mariner from Milton Shore, came before the court in a case about a derelict boat. He had found the ownerless ship of three tons at South Deep, opposite Minster, on the Isle of Sheppey. This vessel he had valued by Richard Reed, Richard Pulter, William Murdock, Thomas Byam, all mariners from Milton, and William Norman, a London mariner. They priced the boat at 30 shillings. Scott made a good profit when he sold the vessel to William Damyn of Foulness Island for 36 shillings and 8 pence. He was ordered to pay half of the purchase money to the Lord High Admiral and give security to the Court for the other half of the money, in case someone claimed the ship within a year and a day.

A case of piracy came before the court in 1540. A London fisherman named Sharp accused a man called Pope from Leigh. Sharp alleged that at Easter, 1539, he was in a peter boat (a type of fishing boat) visiting Leigh to buy supplies. He met Pope, who said, 'come on land'. He landed, thinking that Pope wanted to buy some of his fish.

PARTICULARS

AND

Conditions of Sale,

OF AN UNDIVIDED THIRD PART OR SHARE, OF AND IN

All Those

VALUABLE FREEHOLD

OYSTER LAYINGS & SEA SHORES,

Called Milton Hall, otherwise Middleton Hall, and Prittlewell Priory

SHORES OR SEA GROUNDS,

CONTAINING ABOUT 800 ACRES.

And of and in

A FREEHOLD DWELLING HOUSE,

AND PREMISES, SITUATE AT SOUTHEND,

In the Parish of Prittlewell,

Which will be Sold by Auction, by

MESSRS. JACKSON,

AT THE ROYAL HOTEL, SOUTHEND,

On TUESDAY, August the 15th, 1826,

AT 12 FOR 1 O'CLOCK,

By Direction of the Proprietor.

Particulars, and Conditions of Sale, may be had of Messrs. Wilson and Swaine, Solicitors, Rochford; of Messrs, Berkley, No. 3, Lincoln's Inn; Newcastle Coffee House, and Blue Anchor Tavern, St. Mary at Hill, London; at the Principal Inns Milton, Sheerness, Margate, Gravesend, Rochester; Ipswich; Harwich, Colchester, Brightlingsea, Burnham, Southend, and at the Auctioneers' Offices, Hertford, Chelmsford, and Rochford.

Particulars.

AN UNDIVIDED THIRD PART OR SHARE OF AND IN THOSE HIGHLY

VALUABLE

Freehold Oyster Layings

AND SEA SHORES,

Called Milton Hall, otherwise Middleton Hall, and Prittlewell Priory Shores, or Sea Grounds, containing about 800 ACRES:—And of and in

A FREEHOLD DWELLING HOUSE AND PREMISES,

SITUATE AT SOUTHEND, IN THE PARISH OF PRITTLEWELL,

In the County of Essex.

Mr. EDMUND TAYLOR, has the Occupation of the Shores until the 1st of February next, but possession may be had sooner if required.

The Dwelling House is in the occupation of a Tenant at will at the low rent of £8 per annum

The Shores abound with Native Oyster Brood, Muscles, Cockles, and Perriwinkles. They are distant from London, by Land, or Water, about 40 miles, and extend from Southend, to within a short distance of the Port of Leigh.

There are Two Hard or Road Ways over the Shores, for the convenience of landing passengers, &c. at low water; let at rents amounting to Forty Pounds per annum, with other extensive and valuable priviledges.

THE OYSTERS PRODUCED FROM THESE LAYINGS, ARE OF A SUPERIOR QUALITY, AND FETCH HIGH PRICES AT MARKET.

The Shores also abound with that Valuable Production the ROMAN CEMENT STONE which is obtained in large Quantities with much facility and at a small expence.

When he came ashore Pope hauled the boat on to dry land and stole a peck of fish, which was two gallons worth, leaving Sharp with the residue: 'which were but few and all the smallest and the worst.'

When he asked for payment he was told: 'What! Knave! Shall I never rid the country of you?'

There was evidently a feud between the two men. Sharp's defence was that the fish came from a creek in the manor of Leigh, owned by William Stafford, over which he had rights of jurisdiction.

Milton was noted for her oysters in the 18th and 19th centuries. Large oyster beds were laid in 1770 and remained until 1830, by which time they had fallen into disuse, until disappearing completely around 1850.

Writing in 1786, the historian Philip Morant commented on the large oyster beds on Milton Shore, and described the industry:

'The oysters are bought hither small from the southern coast for this island, particularly from the coast of Sussex and Dorsetshire, where the dredgers employ the poor people to pick them in baskets, in the months of February, March and April, and putting them in their vessels ready to receive them, sail back here, and lay them in the water till they come to their proper growth, which is about seven or eight months. The owners of the oysters here have their proper limits staked out and have an advantage over the rest of the rest of the dredgers in this country, in being so much nearer London. But in a frosty season, the oysters here, from the shallowness if the water, are more liable to be killed by the severity of the weather; the shore being even and dry when the tide is out and not having the conveniency of the pits and layings about Colchester and Maldon, which are replenished with new water almost every tide.'

The reason for the Thames Estuary being so good a feeding ground was attributed by Dr Murie as to

'the shallow waters conducting to a congenial temperature. When their salinity just hits the happy medium, varied by the occasional freshets form the rivers. But the great factors of the oysters thriving and breeding so well in the Thames Estuary and the creeks and waters connected therewith, is the abundance of diatoms, foraminifera and the such like microscopic plants and animals. On the muddy clay, when dry at ebb, there is everywhere a coating of olive-brown, slimy-looking material, otherwise a delicate film of diatoms of various species. Now nothing equals the unctuous blue London clay - locally known as 'clyte' - together with brackish water, for the fostering of these lowly organised algae. Add to this a substratum of gravel and shelly sand, with just sufficient superficial deposit, teeming as it does with microscopic life, and you have a choice home for the sedentary oyster and its molluscan fraternity.

The condition of the coast and rivers of Essex were so conducive to the cultivation of oysters that in their heyday the county supplied 70% of the world's consumption of oysters.

Daniel Scratton and his favourite hounds (*by permission of Southend Museums*)

Glynds, built in the 1600s. Prittlewell Schoolhouse endowed by Daniel Scratton. Demolished 1950s

THE SCRATTON FAMILY

Daniel Scratton
Lord of the Manor
Died at Belstead, Suffolk, 1698, aged 78 years
left estate to nephew
|

Daniel Scratton of Butlers, Broomfield, near Chelmsford
Died without issue and intestate, 2nd June, 1744
|

Contest of relations as to who was next of kin
Decided at Chelmsford Assizes, 1745
Found in favour of
Daniel Scratton of Harkstead, Suffolk
Died 13th July, 1760, aged 55
Married Mary
Died 17th November, 1805, aged 85
Both buried in a vault at St Mary with St Leonard Church,
Broomfield, near Chelmsford
|

| Daniel | John | William | Sarah | Joseph | Thomas | James | Robert | Mary |

Daniel Scratton
Eldest Son
Succeeded Estate
Never Married
Major in West Essex Militia
Resided at Middleton Hall, circa 1788
Died 13th October, 1811, aged 70
Left Estate to youngest brother Robert Scratton

John of Hackney
Died 16th May, 1808, aged 63

William of Ardleigh, Essex
Married Abigail at Sutton Rectory
Died 26th December, 1835, aged 77
Both buried at Broomfield, near Chelmsford

Sarah
Born 1746

Joseph
Lived at Broughton in Huntingdonshire

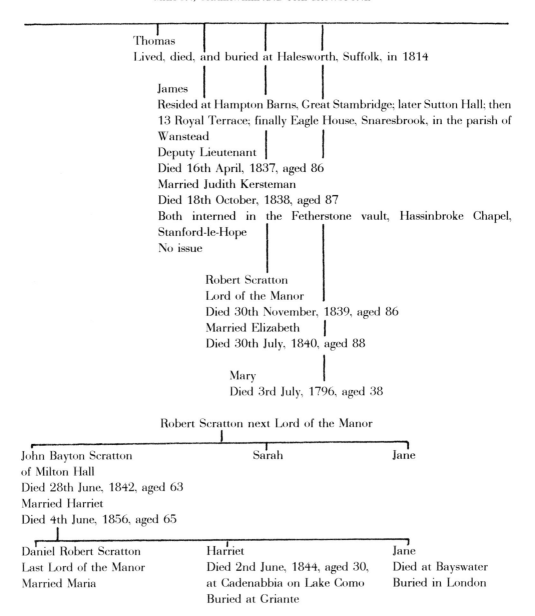

Thomas
Lived, died, and buried at Halesworth, Suffolk, in 1814

James
Resided at Hampton Barns, Great Stambridge; later Sutton Hall; then
13 Royal Terrace; finally Eagle House, Snaresbrook, in the parish of
Wanstead
Deputy Lieutenant
Died 16th April, 1837, aged 86
Married Judith Kersteman
Died 18th October, 1838, aged 87
Both interned in the Fetherstone vault, Hassinbroke Chapel,
Stanford-le-Hope
No issue

Robert Scratton
Lord of the Manor
Died 30th November, 1839, aged 86
Married Elizabeth
Died 30th July, 1840, aged 88

Mary
Died 3rd July, 1796, aged 38

Robert Scratton next Lord of the Manor

John Bayton Scratton	Sarah	Jane
of Milton Hall		
Died 28th June, 1842, aged 63		
Married Harriet		
Died 4th June, 1856, aged 65		

Daniel Robert Scratton	Harriet	Jane
Last Lord of the Manor	Died 2nd June, 1844, aged 30,	Died at Bayswater
Married Maria	at Cadenabbia on Lake Como	Buried in London
	Buried at Griante	

THE BEGINNING OF THE END OF THE MANOR OF MILTON

The Manor of Milton continued practically unchanged until the middle of the 19th century. It was then sold in 1869 for housing by the last Lord of the Manor, Daniel Scratton, being the first estate in the Parish of Prittlewell to be sold for building development. The Scratton family had bought the estate from the descendants of Sir Richard Riche, the Tudor lord and favourite of Henry VII, in the late 17th century. The first member of the Scratton family to own the Estate was also called Daniel Scratton. In Suffolk in the parish of Belstead, where he was buried, there lies an altar tomb bearing the inscription:

'Daniel Scratton, Gentleman of Prittlewell, County of Essex, died 3rd May 1698 aged 78 years.'

The Scratton family was very wealthy and influential and were great benefactors of Prittlewell, donating among other things, in 1727 the land for the first public school in North Street, Prittlewell. This school catered for the poor children of the town, giving education to ten needy children on the condition that they should be taught;

'to read, and write, and instruct them in the catechism and principles of the Christian religion according to the usage of the Church of England.'

In 1739, the Lord of the Manor, Daniel Scratton, made a further donation of land, increasing the North Street site to nearly twenty one acres enabling the free education of sixteen children. The school was described by the Parliamentary Commissioners, reporting from 1819 to 1837 as:

'The premises consist of a house of lath and plaster, situate in the village, near the bridge; it comprises a schoolroom of about 30 ft. in length and 20 ft. in breadth, and several rooms which are appropriated to the use of the schoolmaster.'

The school grew to accommodate the education of between forty to fifty boys and between thirty to forty girls. The children were taught reading, writing, ciphering, and religious knowledge, the girls additional needlework. The school proved very popular growing to one hundred and seventy five pupils in 1872 and outgrowing its site near the village pump in North Street. Prittlewell Church of England School moved to a new site near St Mary's Church in East Street. There is still a Church of England school in East Street, now called St Mary's Prittlewell Church of England School.

The last Lord of the Manor was also called Daniel Scratton. His estate had grown to 2,117 acres with a gross annual value of £1,286 with an additional estate in Devon of 2,639 acres with a gross annual income of £3,000, giving him a total income of £5,000 per annum. A considerable sum, as the schoolmaster of the village school, Prittlewell Church of England School only received in 1836 £23 per year from the school's charity fund, plus an amount not exceeding £30 a year from donations and the collection plate from St Mary's.

Daniel Scratton was a typical squire of the period, loving cricket and hunting. Indeed in 1883 he was so eager to play in a cricket match in which seven sons of a

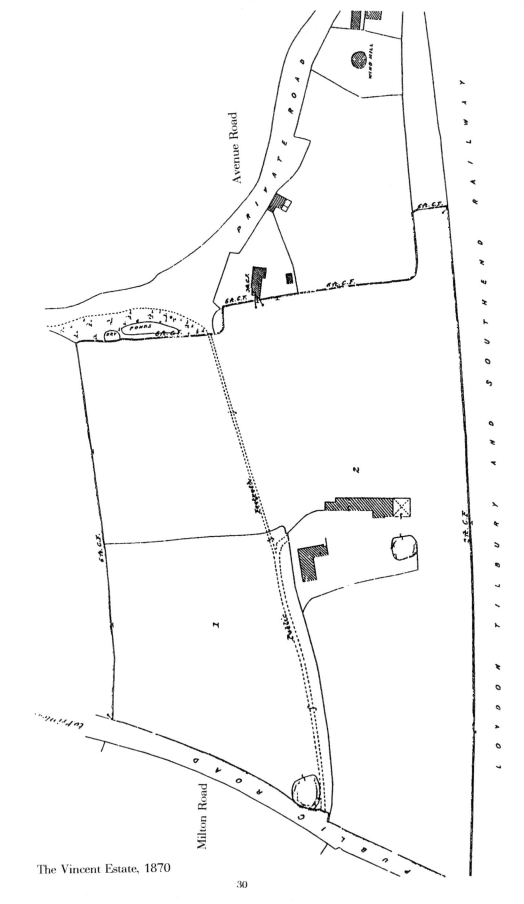

The Vincent Estate, 1870

THIRD PORTION OF THE ESSEX ESTATES

BELONGING TO DANIEL ROBERT SCRATTON, ESQ.

Particulars and Conditions of Sale

OF HIGHLY

Important Freehold Estates,

SITUATE IN THE PARISHES OF

PRITTLEWELL, EASTWOOD, AND GREAT STAMBRIDGE,

COMPRISING

THE "PRIORY,"

A MOST ATTRACTIVE RESIDENCE AT PRITTLEWELL,

WITH

BEAUTIFUL LAWNS AND PLEASURE GROUNDS, WALLED GARDENS, STABLING,

AND A

HANDSOMELY-TIMBERED SMALL PARK;

A SMALLER FAMILY RESIDENCE,

KNOWN AS

"MILTON," OTHERWISE "MIDDLETON HALL,"

WITH

GARDENS, STABLING, COACH HOUSES, FARM PREMISES,

AND

EXCEEDINGLY PRODUCTIVE LAND ADJOINING THERETO,

SEVERAL FIRST-CLASS FARMS,

DWELLING HOUSES AND ACCOMMODATION LAND,

CONTAINING ALTOGETHER

1813 a.   1 r.   15 p.,

Which will be Sold by Auction, by

MESSRS. BEADEL,

AT THE MART, TOKENHOUSE YARD, LONDON,

ON THURSDAY, THE 22ND DAY OF JULY, 1869,

AT TWELVE FOR ONE O'CLOCK, IN NINETEEN LOTS.

Particulars, with Plans and Conditions of Sale, may be obtained of Messrs. GREGSON & SON, Solicitors, Rochford, Essex; at the MART; and of Messrs. BEADEL, 25, Gresham Street, London, E.C.

LOT NINE.

(Colored Blue on Plan)

A MODERATE-SIZED

FAMILY RESIDENCE,

KNOWN AS

"MILTON," OTHERWISE "MIDDLETON HALL,"

Situate fronting the High Road, about midway between SOUTHEND and PRITTLEWELL,

CONTAINING

LAWNS, PLEASURE GROUNDS, SHRUBBERIES,

WITH

LARGE PARTLY-WALLED GARDEN,

Three-Stall Nag Stable, Loose Box, Harness Room, and Carriage Houses with Servants' Room and Lofts over,
Piggeries, Poultry Houses, &c.,

ALSO

CONVENIENT FARM BUILDINGS,

CONSISTING OF

Barn, Stabling for 12 Horses, Enclosed Cattle and Horse Yards with Shedding, and Bullock Stalls, Cow House,
Waggon Lodge, &c.,

AND

TWO ENCLOSURES OF LAND,

STUDDED WITH

FINE WALNUT, OAK, AND OTHER ORNAMENTAL TIMBER,

CONTAINING ALTOGETHER

10 a.   2 r.   37 p.

THIS LOT IS IN HAND, AND POSSESSION MAY BE HAD ON COMPLETION OF THE PURCHASE local Foulness farmer were playing, he drove his four-in-hand coach over the dangerous Broomway Sands at low tide, endangering his life, to play in the match at Foulness. He was a colourful, larger than life character, and could often be seen following the hounds, at his other great passion, hunting. Squire Scratton's love of hunting was well known locally and he was a leading participant, riding with Lord Petre's hounds. He was the Master of the South East Hunt. The Scratton family resided at Prittlewell Priory and Milton Hall.

In 1863 Squire Scratton was presented with a silver inkstand as an appreciation of his services with the Essex Hunt Union. In 1934 the inkstand was purchased by the then Mayor, Councillor H E Frith, and presented to the town in the memory of a great man, the last Squire of Milton.

In 1869 the Estate was sold by Daniel Scratton, for housing and this together with the Cliff Town Estate which was developed for housing by the firm of Brassey, Betts & Co and built by Lucas Bros between 1858-1860, formed the beginning of modern Southend and Westcliff. The first part of the sale was on 29th April, 1869, in sixty seven lots consisting of the area between the shrubbery and the railway in Southend. The sale took three hours to complete, due to questions being asked about the rights to the road in front of Royal Terrace. There was concern at the time of the need to preserve the Shrubbery and allow general access to the residents of the town. The Shrubbery was described in a guide to the town in 1824 as:

'In front of the Terrace (Royal Terrace) there is a fine broad gravel promenade, and between this and the sea is the Shrubbery, which, with a little care, and at a very small expense, might be made into a most delightful resort. It extends the entire length of the Terrace, the descent from which to the beach has been cut into intersecting walks, and planted with a variety of trees. the whole being enclosed with a light fence of posts and rails, with gates and seats at convenient distances. Unfortunately this pleasant little enclosure, which, with a little attention, might be made an ornament and an object of attention, not only to the houses on the Terrace, but to the town itself, has been allowed, in a great measure, to fall to decay, and now deserves more the name of a wilderness than any other appellation; but it is still an agreeable spot, and it is hoped the increasing fame of this sea bathing place will soon induce those who have it in their power to turn the great natural advantages of the Shrubbery to more account.'

The Shrubbery had been allowed to sink into decay and concerned citizens of the town wanted the area to be restored to its former glory with steps taken to assure the parks future maintenance as an attractive asset to Southend. The dispute was eventually settled by the setting up of a body of trustees to administer the care and upkeep of the Shrubbery. The residents of Royal Terrace were requested to pay ten shillings per year for its maintenance and allowed free private access. Entrance to the Shrubbery was by ticket only, the public being charged a daily rate of three pence or an annual subscription of fifteen shillings with a weekly rate of two shilling per family or one shilling singly. In 1918 Southend Corporation acquired the Shrubbery and

A drawing dated 1817 of Milton Hall

Nazareth House, 1930

opened it to the general public free of charge, preserving one of Southend's finest areas of coastline for future generations to enjoy.

The second part of the sale of the Milton Estate was on 29th June, 1869, for the land bounded by Scratton Road, London Road, High Street and Avenue Road, including the cricket field, opposite the Cricketers Inn. This field was sold to Thomas Dowsett, who was the first Mayor of Southend from 1892-3, for £300. Hamlet Mill, advertised as being in 'good working order', was sold to Mr Thomas Arnold for £1,000. It was from the land that was sold at this sale that the Park Estate was built. In the *Southend Standard* of 11th April, 1884, the following appeared showing the large changes that occurred in that occurred in the area as a result of this sale of land:
'The Park Estate, where thirty or even twenty years ago the only houses were Milton Hall, the old Mill House in the Avenue Road, or what was then called Mill Lane or Love Lane, a little low cottage and some farm premises, now the estate is covered with 300-400 houses."

Milton Hall together with approximately ten acres of ground was sold for £2,250 to the Rev J Wonnacott who turned it into a private boarding school which he called Milton Hall School. The school was short-lived, and Rev Wonnacott sold it to the Sisters of Nazareth who changed the name to Nazareth House. In August, 1873, the nuns moved in, converting it to a convent for their Order and a home for the aged and infirm, also destitute children. In October, 1875, the building was enlarged, a new wing added for the children's accommodation, and in 1879 a further wing was built enabling the nuns to care for more old people and children. In 1900 Milton Hall itself was demolished to make way for a new Convent, but the building in London Road is still known as Nazareth House, a living testament to the hard work and dedication of the Sisters of Nazareth. The old name of Milton Hall has faded from the town's memory.

It was in the boundary wall of Nazareth House in the London Road opposite the Park Tavern that there was located what was known locally as a foundling cradle and bell. Abandoned babies were placed in the metal cradle and the basket turned round. This pulled down a metal grill and rang the bell to summon the nuns. The nuns would take the baby, the grille protecting the identity of the parent and guaranteed the anonymity of the source. This was an ideal way for abandoned children to be given into the care of the Sisters of Nazareth. The bell was demolished with the wall when the London Road was widened at the beginning of the century.

The Vincent Estate was sold in 1870. This comprised the area between Milton Road and Avenue Road and Avenue Terrace and the railway line. It was known locally as Vincent's Farm. Avenue Road, one of the boundaries of the farm, was at this time a private road. The old Vincent's Farm is now all covered with housing and the name only remains in St Vincents Road, which was one of the premier roads in the borough. When St Vincents Road was first built the houses were occupied by families with a full staff of servants; many nannies from the road walked their charges in the nearby Southend Park. In the road itself were many high class private schools.

Interior of the chapel, Milton Hall (from *The Architect*, 27th December, 1879)

The remainder of the Milton Hall Estate was sold in December, 1890. This was situated on the northern side of the London Road between North Road and Rochford Road and became known as Milton Hall Farm.

Milton Hall Farm was farmed by Mr George Hart, whose land stretched from what is now Victoria Circus to the Blue Boar Pub, and covered the site occupied by Victoria Station, Victoria Circus Shopping Centre, Victoria Avenue, Baxter Avenue, and Boston Avenue. George Hart was born in 1841 and began farming twenty years later. From his farm he supplied the whole of Southend with milk from his horse-drawn milk cart. After builders bought the land for developing into what was to become the core of modern Southend he moved to Stanbridge Brewery where he continued his dairy farming. He retired in 1890 to Ashingdon Hall. When he died in 1934, aged 93, after nearly a century of local farming it was in his home at 91 Baxter Avenue, a house built on his former farm. He was a well respected man and a keen local church worker, serving his local church, Trinity Church (Reformed Episcopal) and Hawkwell Parish Church as a sidesman.

The Hart family also owned the butchers in Prittlewell called Warren, next to the Spread Eagle Public House. The butchers was housed in one of the oldest buildings in Prittlewell and had a reputation for selling good quality meat. The Spread Eagle Inn itself was on one of the main stopping places of the twice-weekly horse-drawn carriages that left there for Aldgate, London. By 1794 the service had expanded into a daily horse-drawn coach leaving the Bull Inn, Aldgate, and Whitechapel Church, London travelling 41½ miles to Southend, via Rochford and Hadleigh or Leigh and Milton.

Milton House, later known as Shorefields House, was situated in Milton at the western end of the cliffs, where the Cliffs Pavilion now stands. It was a large imposing house with a large garden and views of the meadows which then stretched down to the beach. In the grounds a large mulberry tree bloomed every year, staining the road mauve with its mass of brightly coloured berries.

It was at Shorefields House that Dr Frederick Nolan, Vicar of Prittlewell between 1822 and 1864, resided. Dr Nolan was described by the historian Philip Benton as: 'a very able linguist and learned man, and one of the most accomplished, ripe and masterly scholars in Europe.'

Between 1822 and 1833, Dr Nolan wrote a number of theological books in Shorefields House. Being concerned about the accuracy of his works, he set up his own printing press in the house and employed his own compositor and printer to produce the books. This press was probably the town's first printing press.

It was Dr Nolan who was involved in what became known as 'The Vicar and the Bell Ringers'. An eccentric man of Irish descent he was quick to anger and was known for his fiery temper. He decided to change the time of the church bell-ringing from 5 a.m. to the later time of 8 a.m. This caused resentment by the ringers who objected, preferring the original time and taking a dislike to being told when to ring their bells. Things got so heated that on Sunday morning, 14th June, 1840, between nine and ten

Shorefield House

Pound Cottage, Milton Road (*by permission of Southend Libraries*)

the Vicar tried to cut the bell ropes with a carving knife while the bells were being rung. Pandemonium ensured, the Parson barring the bell-ringers from the church. The police were called to try to pacify the general brouhaha and stop the ringers entering the building. Various summonses and cross-summonses were issued. The parishioners were by now fully incensed and marched to the church breaking the Rectory windows and forcing Dr Nolan to arm himself with pistols to protect himself and his family. The irate parishioners broke into the church and climbed up on to its roof reaching the belfry where chaos reigned, Dr Nolan firing pot shots at them from the vicarage. Five of the ringers were summoned to appear before an ecclesiastical court where heavy fines were imposed on them. One of the men, James Beeson, was arrested and imprisoned at Chelmsford Gaol for thirteen weeks until the fines had been paid by subscription raised by his fellow parishioners. Hatred of Dr Nolan was intense and an effigy was burnt of him at Prittlewell on Guy Fawkes Night by the angry parishioners. The bell ringers had to be bound by oath not to molest the Vicar and leave him in peace.

The exploits of the Vicar and the bell-ringers caught the imagination of the local populace and many satirical songs and skits were published. Perhaps the best known song was the following which was sung to the tune of 'The Mistletoe Bough':

>The village had long been quiet and still,
>The Parson had always enjoyed his will,
>And all his Parishioners feared his frown,
>Looking with awe as he pass'd through the Town.
>The Children all curtsied or made a bow,
>As every Child to a Parson knows how.
>Angelina looked bold as she gazed around,
>Triumphantly striding in haste o'er the ground.
>But Oh, poor Freddy is done, Oh.
>This had long been the case, and 'tis known by us all,
>Each day as they strutted to Middleton Hall [Milton Hall].
>But time alters all things, and so it has here,
>Although the poor Doctor himself thinks its queer;
>For whenever he strutts or parades through the place,
>He is hooted and hissed by each child to his face,
>Though a bludgeon he carries the young brats to chastise,
>They still will continue increasing their cries.
>But Oh, poor Freddy is done, Oh.
>Now the cause is quite clear, tho' the Doctor can't see,
>And yet it has long been detected by me.
>The Sermons he preaches are long threadbare and stale:
>Tho' attentive you listen to hear him you fail.
>Then his brogue, tho' not Irish, none can understand,
>Although he's a native of dear Paddy Land;

39

And should a Friend die, or your Father or Son,
You must have him buried exactly at one.
But Oh, poor Freddy is done, Oh.
To be so respected what Parson could bear?
So resolves he will leave, and thus end the affair;
But a Curate must have, by his rules to abide,
If one can be found to consent to be tied,
That the Bells shall not ring except on condition
The Churchwardens ask the Curate permission.
And if none can be found to consent to this plan,
We still must put up with poor Freddy Nolan.
But Oh, poor Freddy is done, Oh.
Now the Church is deserted, and the Pews nearly bare,
Yet however unwilling, ('tis truth I declare,)
The Bells shall not ring, and no Church Rate shall be,
Until from the Prison James Beeson is free.
Since this is determined, and must be our plan,
When a Meeting is called pray all come to a man;
Be firm, stick to this, and the means may not fail,
For why should a Ringer be shut up in Gaol?
But Oh, poor Freddy is done, Oh.

Another example of Dr Frederick Nolan's stubbornness occurred in 1840. Due to the growing population of Southend it was decided at a meeting held on 27th September, 1832, by the then Bishop of London, Dr Bloomfield, that town needed another church. The Church of St John the Baptist was planned to meet the growing need of churchgoers. Dr Nolan, Vicar of Prittlewell, strongly disagreed, he flew into a rage and argued that his Church of St Mary's at Prittlewell could serve all the parishioners of both Southend and Prittlewell and refused to let the Bishop of London lay the foundation stone. Christopher Parsons noted in his diary on Midsummer Day, Wednesday, 24th June, 1840:

'The Bishop of London came to lay a stone in the new chapel... but Parson Nolan would not let him.'

The Bishop, after many long arguments with the aggravated Dr Nolan gave way and returned to London with the stone remaining unlaid. But the fiery Vicar of Prittlewell eventually lost the quarrel. In 1842 Southend was separated ecclesiastically from Prittlewell and the Church of St John the Baptist was built at a cost of £1,500.

Milton House was later owned by Mr Brown, who had Milton Avenue built. He was said at the time to have built the street to improve his vista from the house and cut out the view of Lydford Road.

The cliffs were very different in the late 19th century to today. They resembled the Downs of Sussex with grassy meadows running down to the beach, and covered in wild flowers, a haven for the numerous rabbits and other animals that inhabited them. The *Southend Standard* of April, 1884, describes the area as:

'The aspect of the cliff is very different from what it was thirty years ago; then the brow was many yards seawards of its present irregular outline, and in addition, it presented if not a more picturesque, certainly a more rural aspect. There were then in abundance the wild flora of English woodland, primroses, violets etc., with numerous members of the rabbit tribe, the nightingale, thrush, lark, and other songsters.'

Unfortunately the maintenance of the cliffs was neglected and erosion caused the area to become unsafe. The cliffs were disintegrating, whole sections of earth were falling on to Southend Esplanade, blocking the road and turning it into a series of small mounts and pitted holes. It was said at the time that:

'One thing all agreed, the houses (west of Royal Terrace), New Town and all, would very shortly subside into the sea.'

Concern was expressed over the safety of Cliff Town Parade. In 1878 the owner, Mr H A Brassey offered to hand over the cliffs with a cheque of £500 to the town so that the area could be made safe. Much to the dismay of the Cliff Town residents the offer was rejected. In the autumn of 1881 a meeting of ratepayers was held by the agitated residents to find a solution to the problem and protect this valuable feature of the town. In 1881 a compromise was reached, the town accepted the cliffs and Mr Brassey's cheque, with the proviso that the owners of Cliff Town should pay between a half and a third the cost of the repairs so vitally needed. In 1885 the dispute was finally resolved, Mr Brassey paid £750 and the other residents £250. The cliffs were at last made safe and passing into the guardianship of the town were landscaped to provide an attractive asset to the region. The flower and rose gardens were later added to enhance this section of the towns coastline, which has given a lot of pleasure to many of the local residents over the years as they sat looking over the flowing Thames.

The Hamlet of Milton's name shortened to 'The Hamlet' in an attempt to sell the houses between Milton Road and Hamlet Court Road, which were built by H A Brassey of the building firm, Brassey, Peto, Betts & Co., as a high class suburban retreat. Hamlet Court itself once stood at the junction of Canewdon Road and Hamlet Court Road. Residents of this notable building included such distinguished persons as Sir Richard Cunliffe Owen, Sir Edwin Arnold (author of *The Light of Asia*) and Robert Williams Buchanan, the poet, satirist and playwright.

So gradually the name of Milton was lost as building speculators preferred the more saleable names of 'The Hamlet' and, later, 'Westcliff-on-Sea', and 'Southend-on-Sea'. The original name of the town remained only as a small memory echoed in the name of a few streets and as the name of a voting ward. The vast farming area that was the Estate of Milton was now almost forgotten until the Milton Conservation Society was formed to protect its heritage.

SOUTHEND PARK

Southend Park occupied five acres of meadow land, bordered on four sides by Park Road, Park Terrace, Park Crescent and Avenue Road, the entrance being in Park Road, directly opposite the end of Queens Road.

It was a private park owned by Mr William Steward who charged a sixpenny entrance fee. The park covered an area of about five acres of meadow with a large pond in the south-western corner. It was a very popular place with the town's residents and crowds flocked to use the many sporting facilities that were there and stroll among the green lawns and flower beds.

In 1875 the park had a seven foot wide cinder track used for racing penny farthing bicycles. Other facilities included football and cricket pitches. In 1867 the Rochford Hundred Cricket Club played there before moving to the cricket field that was then in North Road and from there to the Kursaal on the sea front. It was this club that became Southend Cricket Club in 1895 and played from Southchurch Park.

The park became very popular and Mr Steward began making improvements. The pond in the south-western corner was enlarged and two extra lakes in the shape of parallelograms were planned to create an 800 ft long ice rink for winter and a boating lake for summer. Unfortunately the extra ponds never materialised, but according the *Southend Standard,* Mr Steward planted 'large banks of shrubs and evergreens intersected with gravel walks, with seats and rustic summer houses'. The cinder track was widened to 15 feet with easy corners on an 86 foot radius, measuring just over three laps of the track to the mile.

The works were noted in the *Southend Standard* in January, 1881:
Those who were accustomed to see only waste ground last summer will meet with a welcome surprise this year as no pains have been spared to make the whole a charming spot. Boats upon the lake and numerous seats in different parts for viewing cricket matches or bicycle races added in no small degree to the attractiveness of the new Southend Park.'

In the winter of 1880/81, the weather was so cold that the lake in the park froze over sufficiently to permit ice skating, the rink being large enough to accommodate 1,500 skaters. The event was reported in the *Southend Standard* of 21st January, 1881:
'In the evening of Monday (21st January, 1881) that the portion of the park surrounding the lake was illuminated by a considerable number of lamps which were suspended at intervals during the evening. Large fires were also lighted in several places and altogether the scene that was presented was a very lively one, and rendered the more so by the flitting forms of skaters of both sexes who seemed thoroughly to enjoy the exercise.'

The water of the lake was supplied by a natural spring, channelled into an area of about an acre, surrounded by an artificial bank. The lake was kept well stocked with

"THE PARK,"
SOUTHEND-ON-SEA.

PARTICULARS & CONDITIONS OF SALE

OF THE

VALUABLE FREEHOLD PROPERTY,

KNOWN AS

"SOUTHEND PARK,"

Which occupies a most desirable position in the centre of SOUTHEND, a rapidly increasing and improving
SEA-SIDE RESORT, on the Eastern Coast; and embraces an area of about

5 Acres, 0 Roods, 26 Perches,

Which is beautifully timbered and planted with Shrubs and Evergreens, and is tastefully laid out as a

RECREATION GROUND,

Including famous Cricket and Lawn Tennis Grounds, Bicycle Track, Trotting Ring, and excellent accommodation
for Dancing, Skating, Athletic Sports, and Gymnastic Exercises,

ORNAMENTAL WATER

And FISH PONDS, which are well stocked with Tench, Carp, Dace, and Gold Fish;

WHICH WILL BE SOLD BY AUCTION, BY

MR. CLEAR,

On TUESDAY, September 20th, 1881,

AT THE AUCTION MART, TOKENHOUSE YARD,

BANK, LONDON,

At One o'clock precisely, by direction of the Proprietor, in ONE Lot.

Particulars and Conditions of Sale, with Lithographed Plan, may be obtained at the Auction Mart,
London; of Messrs. DIGBY & EVANS, Solicitors, Maldon, Essex; and of Mr. CLEAR, Auctioneer and
Estate Agent, Maldon, Essex.

RICHARD POOLE, PRINTER, MALDON

PARTICULARS.

THE VALUABLE

FREEHOLD PROPERTY

Known as

"SOUTHEND PARK,"

Which embraces an area of about 5A., 0R., 26P., is beautifully timbered and planted with shrubs and evergreens, and is tastefully laid out as a

RECREATION GROUND,

Including famous Cricket and Lawn Tennis Grounds, Bicycle Track, Trotting Ring, and excellent accommodation for Skating, Dancing, Athletic Sports, and Gymnastic Exercises.

The grounds are encircled with a belt of beautiful evergreens, and are intersected with ornamental water, fish ponds, &c., which afford accommodation for 1500 skaters in the winter season.

The Fish Ponds are well stocked with tench, carp, dace, and goldfish, and furnish excellent sport for Anglers during the summer months.

The water is supplied from a never-failing spring which rises upon the Property.

A Luncheon Marquee and Storehouse in the rear, erected upon the Property, will be included in the sale.

SOUTHEND PARK is enclosed with newly-erected brick walls and fences, is surrounded with excellent roads, and occupies a most important position in the centre of Southend; although recently opened as a recreation ground it has already become a necessity to the Town and Neighbourhood, and produces large profits, and if further developed must eventually become a most lucrative investment, and would now readily command a Rent of

£200 : 0 : 0 PER ANNUM,

The Proprietor is a Builder and Contractor in a large way of business, at Southend, and consequently is unable to devote the necessary time and attention to the development of "Southend Park," and is therefore desirous of selling the Property.

Possession will be given on completion of the Purchase.

Southend is rapidly increasing in magnitude and importance and is daily becoming one of the most fashionable SEA-SIDE RESORTS on the Eastern Coast.

carp, tench, adduce and goldfish. Anglers paid an extra one shilling a day to fish in the lake and spectators paid threepence to watch from the promenade

On 13th March, 1881, the *Southend Standard* announced:
The bicycle route will be opened in Easter Monday when a special contest will take place, open to all England. Three silver cups will be awarded as 1st, 2nd, and 3rd prizes to the winners. Application for entries and other information may be had of Mr H Dennis, Park Tavern, Cliff Town; Mr W Steward, 28 Park Street.'

In fact many fêtes and galas were held in Southend Park, including the annual Grand Agricultural Gala, with fireworks and cycle races and other spectaculars including one advertising a 'monster balloon'. These fêtes were very popular, the park ringing with the sound of people enjoying themselves.

One man writing in a letter about his boyhood in Southend remembered Southend Park well. Reminiscing, he wrote:
'Mother used to take us and I can remember a cycle around the park with the penny farthing bikes. They had canvass all around the park and we would find a place from outside where we would see without paying to get in.'

In 1881 the park was offered for sale to Southend Corporation for £800, but the offer was refused and Mr Steward sold the land privately for £2800.

The park continued for a while afterwards before eventually the land was used for housing. The new housing merged in with the existing Park Estate and today only the names of the streets give a clue to where was sited one of Southend's premier parks, a green oasis lost to the town for ever.

THE SOUTHEN

SOUTHEND PARK,
SOUTHEND-ON-SEA.

Bicycle Handicaps

EASTER MONDAY, APRIL 18th.

A FIVE-MILE HANDICAP.

First Prize, A STERLING SILVER CUP, value £7 10s.; Second Prize, £3 10s. ; Third Prize, £1 10s.

A ONE-MILE HANDICAP

First Prize, £4; Second Prize, £2; Third Prize, £1.

The above are open to Gentlemen Amateurs of any recognised Bicycle Club, or friends introduced by Members of such. Entrance Fee 2s. 6d. for each event. Entries with Fee to be sent to Mr. W. STEWARD, 28, Park Street, Southend, on or before Saturday, April 9th, 1881 ; stamps only received 1s for 1s.

The Prizes will be on View at Mr. Dennis's, Cliff Tavern, Southend.

FIRST HEAT AT ONE O'CLOCK.

J. Jackson, Esq., has kindly consented to distribute the Prizes.

ROCHFORD HUNDRED FOOTBALL CLUB RACES.

In order that there may be no excuse for the physical powers of the Athletes in this neighbourhood to in any way degenerate between the Football and Cricket seasons, the R.H.F.C. have arranged some

ATHLETIC SPORTS
FOR
WEDNESDAY, APRIL 6th,
IN THE
SOUTHEND PARK,

By the kind permission of the Proprietor (Mr. W. Steward), who is working in conjunction with the R.H.F.C. to make it a success.

All who wish to enter for the following events may apply to Mr. E. H. Benton, Great Wakering.

(OPEN TO THE R.H.F.C.) Viz:—Quarter of a mile and 100 yards Flat Races, 120 yards Hurdle Race (10 flights), Long and High Jumps, and Consolation Race.

(OPEN TO ALL AMATEURS): — One mile and 220 yards Flat Races, throwing the Cricket Ball, five miles Bicycle Race (to be run on a track), and a Steeple-chase (? mile.)

ENTRANCE FEE to each event is 2s. 6d. to outsiders, and 1s. to R.H.F.C. Entrances Close March 29th.

HAMLET COURT

By the beginning of the 20th century the area of the hamlet of Milton became known as simply The Hamlet. One of the main buildings was an imposing house known as Hamlet Court, the mansion which gave its name to Hamlet Court Road

Hamlet Court was a distinctive large house set back in its own extensive grounds bordering Hamlet Court Road, Ditton Court Road and Canewdon Road. It was a large, well proportioned house and both the house and grounds were screened from the road by large chestnut trees, giving the property complete privacy from prying eyes. The *Southend Standard* of 29th October, 1925, described the house thus:

'It is a substantially built house of two storeys, with spacious cellar and loft; the walls, of red brick, are in places of unusual thickness: on the north side they are covered with stucco. The house comprises two wings, with a central porch of timber on the south side, and stands on about two acres of ground. The roof is of red tiles. There is a front and a back staircase; the rooms are numerous, but none are of large size; several are crossed by thick oaken beams in the roof. The south front is entirely covered by a vine: that is of great age is proved by the fact that the grandfather of Mr William Boosey of Rochford used to speak of the days spent by him trimming it. Although standing back but a few yards from Hamlet Court Road, the house and gardens preserve a delightful flavour, and there are glasshouses in which many magnificent chrysanthemums have been grown.'

Hamlet Court had many distinguished residents among whom were the notable Sir Philip Cunliffe Owen, Director of the South Kensington Science Museum, and the authors, Sir Edwin Arnold and Robert Buchanan.

Sir Edwin Arnold was a one time Principal of a Government College at Poona, India, and later edited the *Daily Telegraph*. He lived in Hamlet Court, Westcliff, from 1878. A prolific writer in prose and verse he is best remembered for his poem *The Light of Asia*, which he was inspired to write while living at Hamlet Court. Published in 1879 the poem dealt in detail with the life and teachings of Buddha and was hailed as a scholarly literary study of the philosophy of Buddhism. The poem was very popular with readers and over sixty editions in England and eight in America were published, with many foreign translations. It was acknowledged to be a valuable work of great learning, showing a love and understanding of this important faith.

He had strong links with Southend, but his mother's family came from Hockley. Born in Gravesend in 1832, the author moved with his family to a farm at Southchurch Wick when he was fifteen years old. It was at the farm that the budding author started to build up his love of nature, a wonder of which shone through all his work. At the age of twenty five he received an appointment in India where he remained for five years, gaining high office. He put the experiences he learned there to good use, later writing a number of eminent books on the British Raj in India.

Sir Edwin Arnold had a distinguished career and, at the death of Lord Tennyson in 1892, he was held in such high esteem that he was considered as a candidate to the Poet Laureateship that was now available. When he died in 1904, after a long and memorable career, it was a sad loss to the literary world.

Robert Buchanan (1841-1901) was another literary resident of Hamlet Court. A renowned poet, dramatist and novelist of his day. It was at Hamlet Court that Buchanan wrote his famous poem *The City of Dreams* in 1888. A copious writer of poems and prose, he wrote, amongst others, the then highly praised but now forgotten novel *Andromeda*, a story about Canvey Island.

Robert Buchanan was a great lover of Southend and had made frequent visits to the town from 1882 where he and his wife, Mary stayed in Cliff Town Parade, before becoming a permanent resident in 1884 when he moved into Hamlet Court. He was devoted to his wife who was dying from cancer and he thought that Southend's sea air would help restore her health. Unfortunately that hope was in vain, his wife suffered a relapse. She was in constant agony, the pain was intense, and she stoically refused to have pain killing morphine injections. When she finally died in November, 1882, in her husband's arms, Buchanan was overcome with intense grief. Mary Buchanan was buried in St John the Baptist's churchyard, Southend. Her distraught husband dedicated his next book of poems in her memory. The dedication ran as follows:

'To Mary. Weeping and sorrowing, yet in a sure and certain hope of a heavenly resurrection, I place these poor flowers of verse on the grave of my beloved wife, who with the eyes of truest love and tenderness watched these growing over more than twenty years.

Robert Buchanan, Southend, 1882.'

After his wife's sad death Robert Buchanan travelled for a few months to France and before residing in London. He continued to make frequent trips to Southend often accompanied by his companion, G R Simms. Mr Simms wrote about one of these trips: 'Once at Southend we went to bed at three o'clock. At half past eight he was up and ready for a stroll before breakfast. We walked about Southend for an hour. Suddenly my companion left me, saying, 'Go back to the hotel; I will be with you directly.' When he came in I noticed that the knees of his trousers were covered in chalk. He had gone to the graveyard to see the grave of his wife. He had found the gate locked and had climbed the wall.'

In 1884 Robert Buchanan moved permanently to Southend, residing in Hamlet Court. Describing the house as:

'This house which already had been the home of Sir Richard Cunliffe Owen and Sir Edwin Arnold, was a quaint old country place with extensive gardens and eight acres of meadow '

It was from here that the poet wrote:

'There is no lovelier spot when spring becomes a certainty'.

But the house and grounds were already starting to show signs of neglect, the town beginning to make inroads on the expansive gardens, for Robert Buchanan's biographer,

Hamlet Court

Nazareth House

his sister-in-law, Miss Harriet Jay, writing in 1903, said:

'The builder has been busy and Hamlet Court is no longer what it was. In those days it was a paradise to dream in, but now the fine old elms which formed the avenue, known as 'Lovers Walk', have disappeared and in the eight acres of meadow stands the fashionable Queen's Hotel. There is a station too, and the little hamlet is known as Westcliff-on-Sea.'

This was one of the first references to the change of name from the hamlet of Milton to the town of Westcliff-on-Sea.

After two or three years Robert Buchanan moved to Byculla House on the Cliffs. Buchanan had become a very popular author and his plays became particularly in demand. The success of his stage works forced him to move from his beloved town to Maresfield Gardens, South Hampstead.

But Buchanan always kept his love of Southend. When his mother died in 1894 he had her buried next to his wife in St John the Baptist churchyard. A distraught son, he recorded his feelings of loss in his diary which reads:

'At 11 a.m. to-day, after several days of suffering, my beloved mother died, leaving me heart broken. Worn out with days and nights of watching I was dazed and stupefied. O, mother, mother, if we are never to meet again, the whole universe contains nothing to live for! But we must, we shall!'

Later he added:

'I have laid her to rest at Southend, in a beautiful graveyard by the sea, close to the place where she used to be very happy.'

Robert Buchanan died in June, 1901, and was buried next to his adored wife and mother in St John the Baptist's Churchyard, in his beloved town of Southend.

The last owners of Hamlet Court were Mr and Mrs S H Rugg and this fine house was demolished in 1929. The land was split up and sold to various builders who erected shops and housing on the site. In 1925 a building plot with a frontage of 126 feet and a depth of 105 feet was sold for £17,000. Five years later in 1929 a larger plot of land in front of the old house extending from Hamlet Court Road along Canewdon Road to Ditton Court Road was sold by Messrs. Street and Creaser for £40,000. Gradually all the land was sold for redevelopment.

This marked a turning point in the town. All the new shops and houses were sold under the new name of Westcliff-on-Sea. Interestingly, when the railway came to be built, the last station to be named was that of Westcliff. Perhaps the area was still known popularly by its old name of Milton and there was confusion over the title of the district. Anyway, the new name of Westcliff was adopted for the station and the older Milton faded away. The old name of the Hamlet of Milton with all its long links the past is now disregarded. Only a small echo is left in the name of Hamlet Court Road. Hamlet Court itself has become the forgotten house of Southend, its history lost to modern residents of the town.

Western Esplanade, 24th August, 1914 *(reproduced by courtesy of the Essex Record Office)*

Palmeira Arches, 20th March, 1911 *(reproduced by permission of the Essex Record Office)*

THE CRICKETERS' INN

The Cricketers' Inn in London Road has enjoyed an eventful past. It not only housed one of the town's first fire services, but was also where Southend's youngest ever Mayor was born and raised. The Inn has played an important part in the story of the development of the town.

The earliest record of the London Road site is 25th March, 1870, when Rebecca Olley, who wanted to erect and run her own inn, started negotiations for a mortgage of £100 from George Wood to finance her dream. On the 23rd September, 1870, in anticipation of her forthcoming wedding to William Brown, these negotiations were finalised, and Rebecca and William were married on 24th September, 1874. But problems arose when Rebecca's benefactor, George Wood, died on the 15th November, 1877, with the mortgage still outstanding. It was discovered that:

'...no legal mortgage of the said hereditaments and premises to which the muniments of title referred ... was ever executed'.

It appeared that the mortgage was no longer valid; Rebecca was in danger of losing the inn that she had worked so hard for. The problem was resolved by the offer of Walter Gray to purchase the land and house for £1,700. George Olley, William Brown and Rebecca considered the proposal and declared that it was an 'advantageous offer'. It was a chance they could not turn down and they arranged the mortgage to be repaid out of it. Thus was the Cricketers' Inn born, the name coming from the frequent cricket matches played on the playing fields then opposite the tavern.

The Cricketers' Inn was insured on the 24th June, 1924, to midsummer, 1925, for:

Buildings	£10,000
Landlord fixtures and fittings	£1,000
Stables with loft over	£100
Adjoining stable	£100
Architects and surveyors fees	£600
Fences and gates around property	£100

The publican of the Cricketers' Inn in the earlier 1900's, Alec White, Senior, was second-in-command of what was then known as the Southend Volunteer Fire Brigade, the forerunner of the town's present fire service. The horse-drawn fire engine was housed in the yard at the rear of the inn, with the horse's harness suspended over the horse for a quick getaway. It was said with pride by the firemen, that they could be away to fight a fire in less that a minute. Jennie, the name that the men gave the horse that pulled the fire engine, was a small Shetland pony. 'She was small but, by George, she was a goer', remembered his son, Alec, many years later. Fighting fires was thirsty work and the firemen would meet after tackling blazes at the bar of the Cricketers' for a well earned drink.

In 1908 the volunteer firemen won a trophy at the National Union Competitions at Scarborough. It was a great event for the town and there was much excitement as the town welcomed the championship firemen home. They were met at Southend Central Railway Station by a packed crowd. The atmosphere was described by a contemporary local newspaper as: 'deafening cheers and ecstatic excitement.'

They rode through the town on a decorated horse-drawn carriage, there were fireworks and a brass band played. The firemen were escorted by a torchlight procession. The atmosphere was electric with the enthusiastic crowds waving banners with 'Welcome, Champion Firemen of England,' and 'Westcliff is proud of you' written on them. At the bandstand the band of the Oxford Light Infantry played 'See the conquering hero comes'. There had never been so much excitement in the town, people were pleased to welcome home their well deserved heroes after the firemen's spectacular win.

When Alec White, Senior, died in 1912, the Fire Brigade put his coffin on the horse-drawn fire-engine which was used as a hearse, as a mark of respect to a great man. It was the end of an era.

It was that noted firemen's son, also called Alec White, who became Southend's youngest ever mayor and its 16th Freeman. Alec White, Junior, was born and bred in the Cricketers' Inn. He became Southend's youngest ever Councillor in 1931 and Mayor in 1935-1936. He was a colourful and much loved figure of the town. His hobby was conjuring and he took a delight in brightening up official occasions with conjuring tricks, sometimes by producing a string of sausages out of fellow dignitaries pockets. When on Christmas Day, during his term as Mayor of Southend, he was visiting the children's ward of Southend Hospital, he made the children laugh by producing a white rabbit out his top hat, which Mayors then wore on all official occasions.

He was a strong champion of the town and was one of the main supporters of the need for modern entertainment in Southend. On the 20th January, 1965, he was made the 16th Freeman of Southend for his services to the community at the Cliffs Pavilion, which he was instrumental in getting built. When he died in 1972, aged 81, having served the Council for 35 years, it was a sad loss for the town, which lost one of its most respected and colourful citizens. One of Southend's lifeboats was named after him as a tribute to his hard work in the community.

By 1934 the Cricketers' Inn was managed by E I Short and Co. Ltd., they being one of the few landlords of Gray's Pubs to be successful enough to become a limited company. On 29th September, 1933, Timothy O'Riordan leased the Inn for fourteen years and ran the pub successfully throughout the upheaval of the Second World War.

In 1945 Timothy O'Riordan and his wife went for a well deserved holiday to Ireland. Sadly while there, Tim died, and his wife, Nelly O'Riordan returned home alone. Nelly ran the pub on her own until her brother, Frederick Charles Spring and his wife, Dorothy, moved from London to help her. When Nelly died in 1949, Frederick continued to run the pub with his son, Frederick Victor Spring, and in 1953 they became joint licensees; the Inn was run by the same family for 50 years.

The Cricketers' Inn was the heart of the community. Weekly dances were held in the adjoining dance hall. In the 1940s and 50s many people met their future spouses at the popular dances held at the Cricketers'.

In 1973 a mentally deranged man set fire to himself in the bar of the inn. It was after this macabre incident that odd things started occurring in the pub, the Cricketers' Inn being haunted by a poltergeist. Furniture and ornaments were found upturned on the floor and on one occasion every drawer in the kitchen was opened to its fullest extent and every cupboard door open at 90 degrees. No explanation was ever found for these supernatural occurrences and these ghostly happenings continued for a while until the inn was redecorated, when they stopped as suddenly as they had started. The poltergeist had left and the inn regained its former peace.

The Cricketers' Inn still plays a large part in the community today, being one of the oldest and historic inns in Southend. Few of the town's pubs can have had such a colourful past.

Cricketers' Corner (Public House on right) (*reproduced by permission of the Essex Record Office*)

THE CHURCHES OF MILTON CONSERVATION AREA

THE GROWTH OF METHODISM AND PARK ROAD METHODIST CHURCH

Methodism came to the area in the 18th century when its founder, John Wesley, visited Leigh. He made six trips to preach his message at Leigh between 1748 and 1756. His first visit on 12th November, 1748, Wesley describes as:
'I set out for Leigh in Essex. It has rained hard in the former part of the night, which was succeeded by a sharp frost, so that most of the road was like glass; and the north east wind sat just in our face. However, we reached Leigh by four in the afternoon. Here was once a deep, open harbour, but the sands have long since blocked it up and reduced a once flourishing town to a small ruinous village. I preached to most of the inhabitants of the place in the evening, to many in the morning, and then rode back to London.'

It was said that he stayed at the home of Dr Cook, a physician and writer, who was a regular contributor to the *Gentleman's Magazine*, a popular periodical of the day. Dr Cook's house was situated in the town on the south side of the railway. Rev. Wesley's description of his lodgings tallies with what was known of Dr Cook's home. When the Doctor died in 1777, his house was said to be haunted.

Rev John Wesley visited Leigh again on 18th December, 1749, and in 1750. On 12th November, 1753, he returned in a chaise from London to take the service at Leigh, preaching in a very cold draughty room. It was said he again stayed at Dr Cook's house where it was also very cold. Wesley described the visit in his journal as:
'I rode to Leigh, in Essex, and spoke in as awakening a manner as I could. On Wed. Dec. 20th, I left the little flock in peace and love, and cheerfully returned to London. On Mon., Dec. 10th, 1750, I rode to Leigh, in Essex, when I found a little company seeking God, and endeavoured to encourage then in provoking one another to love and good works. Nov. 12th 1753, - I set out in a chaise for Leigh, having delayed my journey as long as I could. I preached at 7, but was extremely cold all the time, the wind coming strong from a door behind, and another on one side; so that my feet felt just as if I had stood in cold water. Tues. 13th, the chamber wherein I sat, though with a large fire, was much colder than the garden, so that I could not keep myself tolerably warm, even when I was close to the chimney.'

The cold turned out to be damaging to his health, and Wesley, who was already ill, returned to London with a pain in his left breast, a violent cough, and a slow fever. He soon recovered and was able to resume his preaching within four days.

On October 27th, 1755, he returned to Leigh. In his diary Wesley gives the following description of the difficulties of travelling in the 18th century:
'We set out for Leigh, in Essex, but being hindered a little in the morning the night came on, without moon or stars, when we were two miles short of Rayleigh. The ruts were so deep and uneven that the horses could scarce stand, and the chaise was

continually in danger on overturning; so that my companions thought it best to walk to town, though the road was both wet and dirty. Leaving them at Rayleigh, I took horse again. It was so thoroughly dark that we could not see our horses' heads; however, by the help of Him to Whom the night shineth as day, we hit every turning, and without going a quarter of a mile out of out way, before nine we came to Leigh. Wednesday 29th, I returned to London.'

Rev. John Wesley's last recorded journey to Leigh was on 11th October, 1756. In his diary he recounts the visit:

'Where we dined, a poor woman came to the door with two little children; they seemed half starved, as well as their mother, who was also shivering with an ague. She was extremely thankful for a little food, and still more so for a few pills, which seldom fail to cure that disorder.'

A highly compassionate man, Wesley also found time to read Voltaire's *Henriade* between his charitable acts in the town on this occasion.

The first Wesleyan chapel was built in Leigh in 1811. On October 11th of that year the following agreement was issued on a piece of land 40 ft by 20 ft: 'to be subject to the Methodist Conference for the term of sixty-one years, ending Oct. 11th 1882, at a yearly rent of £1.1s.'

Unfortunately the land was compulsory purchased in 1854 for the building of the new railway past the town. However, a new Wesleyan chapel was built. During the period between the demolition of the old chapel and the building of the new one services were held in the open air, often to the opposition of the local residents. On one occasion constables were sent 'to pull the preacher down.'

Leigh had its own Wesleyan circuit in 1810, but from 1823 to 1846 it was attached to Chelmsford and, from 1847 to 1853, Maldon. When the quarterly meeting was held in Maldon in 1853 a local preacher complained that the journey to Leigh was too far to walk and asked for a separate local church and a new circuit. A new circuit was created, including Hadleigh, Leigh, Rochford, and Southend. Inquiries were made about 'the cost of a young man'. A new minister was found and given the stipend of £55 per year.

Premises for the new Wesleyan congregation were hard to find. The first services were held in a loft over a coal yard. Between December, 1840, and January, 1843, various other premises in the parish of Prittlewell were registered by the by the Commissionary Court of the Bishop of London as being used by the fledgling Methodist community for religious purposes.

By 1860 it was decided that 'The New Town' of Southend should have its own church. The congregation, which then numbered forty members, met for services in a house near the Army and Navy Inn. By 1868 the congregation was conducting their services in a marquee on Runwell Terrace Green, where a large number of visitors and residents gathered to worship. Unfortunately, the marquee was blown down in one of the gales that plagued that area and new, more permanent premises were sought.

In 1870 Mr J G Baxter gave the congregation the site where Park Road Methodist Church still stands. Mr Henry Cater had built the chapel and school for which he donated the full cost of the building. The chapel was built in 1872 at a cost of £2,500. In 1902 a church hall was built, which also doubled as a school room.

Park Road Methodist Church was the first permanent Methodist Church to be built in Southend. Philip Morant, the local historian, described the church in his book *The History of Rochford Hundred* in 1888 as:

The new Wesleyan Methodist chapel, erected in Park Road, New Town, in 1872, is one of the greatest architectural ornaments of Southend. The exterior is in good taste, and has a very substantial appearance. The style of architecture is early Gothic, the shape is Cruciform, and it is built of Kentish rag stone.

In 1926 the Park Road Methodist Church became the head of the Southend Methodist Circuit. In the minutes of the quarterly meeting of the Southend and Leigh Wesleyan Circuit of 17th March, 1926, the estimated value of the church and its various asserts were;

Church, School and House	£15,000
10 Park Road	£500
18 St Vincents Road	£15,000

The membership had by then increased to 221 adults and 20 juniors, what a difference today! The church buildings were extended over the years to the present size.

In 1970 the church celebrated its century with a celebratory festival of music. The *Southend Standard* of the 7th May, 1970, ran the following:

'Park Road Methodist Church begins its centenary celebrations with a festival of music at the church of May 16th. Southend Philharmonic Orchestra, conducted by George Mowatt, will play pieces by Mozart and Beethoven and the programme will include a festival march, specially composed for the occasion by a member of the church, Mr Arthur Marshall.'

Park Road Methodist Church still stands today and holds regular services despite now having a smaller congregation.

New Wesleyan Chapel, Southend:
Revd John Holland Brown, Minister

THE GROWTH OF BAPTISM AND AVENUE ROAD CHURCH

The first Baptist services were held in Prittlewell in 1823-1824 at the home of Mr Warren, being conducted once a fortnight. By 1854 the Baptist services had been transferred to the home of Anthony Smith in Southchurch. Mr Smith was a local thatcher and gardener, who worked in Shopland. Southend at this time had only two buildings authorised for worship, a church and a chapel. The chapel was situated on the junction of Clarence Street and the High Street and was erected in 1806. It was closed in 1864 when the congregation moved to Cliff Town Church which was built a year later. There is a plaque today in the rear of the High Street depicting where this historic building stood. The church was the Church of St John the Baptist which was built in 1842 and still stands. But neither of these religious establishments served the Baptist faith.

Southend at this time was renowned for its healthy climate. In 1854 John Sutton moved to the town from Islington, London, to take advantage of the restorative sea air. An ardent Baptist, he rode into Prittlewell to find where the local services were held. Asking the village barber where the 'truth was preached' he found that there was only two places of worship, neither of them Baptist. Unable to believe that this was the case he asked the local shoemaker for further information. The shoemaker replied:

'The truth, sir, truth, sir, if you are searching for that, you will not find it in Prittlewell! If you go to Southchurch, about two and a half miles from here, you will find a few poor people who meet in a room and one of the brethren speaks to them.'

He then added: 'Sir, are you a speaker?'

John Sutton replied: 'No, I am only a poor groaner.'

The next Sunday Sutton went to the service held at Anthony Smith's house in Southchurch. He was so impressed with the quality of the preaching that at the first collection he donated eight crowns, enough to buy the minister a black suit.

The first Baptist Church in Prittlewell was built in East Street by Mr Sutton's generosity. He also endowed five cottages worth £300, one for the minister, the other four to be let as an income for the church, any surplus to be given to the poor of Thundersley and Prittlewell Churches. The new church was widely supported by the residents of the growing area as shown by the wide ranging addresses and occupations of the first six trustees who were: James Finch, of Rayleigh, gentlemen; William Westhorp, Great Wakering, Grocer; Samuel Frost, Great Wakering, baker; Joseph Pease, jun., Rayleigh, farmer; George Sneezum, Rayleigh, baker; William Webb, South Benfleet, grocer.

Unfortunately this arrangement did not provide enough of an income for Anthony Smith, who became the first pastor, to live on. He had to supplement his earnings by carrying water around the town. This displeased the brethren, who thought it was demeaning and did not allow the minister enough time to devote to his pastoral duties and they raised the Pastor's salary to a living wage.

Anthony Smith was an eccentric man who was best described by J W Burrows in his book *Southend and District Historical Notes* as:

'It is said of Smith that he preached in a scull cap, had a sounding board hanging over his head, though the ceiling of the chapel was very low, and often sat down in the pulpit after having spoken for a few minutes, declaring that the matter ceased to flow.'

Pastor Smith continued to be the minister of Prittlewell Baptist Church for over twenty years and a memorial was erected in his name in the churchyard in 1874. In 1893 the chapel was demolished to make way for a new building that was erected at a cost of £527. A further extension was added thirteen years later at a cost of £400.

By 1875 it was felt that Southend needed its own Baptist Church. In the *Southend Standard* of Friday, 13th August, 1875, the following appeared:

'With a view to the formation of a Baptist Church in Southend, a few friends have arranged to hold Sunday services in the Town Hall commencing on Sunday, June 6th, 1875, and to be continued until further notice.'

On the 6th June, 1875, the Southend Baptist Church was formed and a year later thirteen brethren and sisters joined hands with Rev J Wigner in fellowship. Three weeks later, the first meeting of members occurred at No. 8 Belmont Villa, Cambridge Road. In August, 1876, an iron building was purchased for £650 on the corner of Princes Street and Hamlet Road, the present site of St Marks Church, and on the 6th September, 1876, the Baptist Tabernacle was opened. Six people were baptised at the Tabernacle's first baptismal service on 5th March, 1877, and on the 25th June, 1878, Rev J Wilson of Pastors College became the first pastor.

Unfortunately, after four years a split developed between Rev. Wilson and the deacons of the church. The Pastor wanted open membership of the church, but the deacons held to the trust deed in favour of 'Closed Membership'. In 1882 the Rev Wilson vacated the pastorate and with many of the church members set up a rival congregation, worshipping once again in the Town Hall and from there to what became Clarence Road Baptist Church.

In October, 1882, the Deacons of the Hamlet Road Baptist Tabernacle offered the pastorship to the Rev H W Childs of Sudbury in Suffolk, who accepted the position. A more permanent building was built at a cost of £950 and dedicated on 14th December, 1885, by the Rev Charles Spurgeon.

In 1900 a large piece of land was purchased at the corner of Milton Road and Avenue Terrace. It was here that the Avenue Road Baptist Church was built, then the largest Baptist building in the Borough, at a cost of £800. On 25th May, 1901, a farewell service was held at the Tabernacle at Hamlet Road. The old building was sold to the Church of England and renamed St Marks, as it is today.

The Avenue Road Baptist Church was badly damaged when it was hit by a bomb on 10th December, 1943, the roof was blown off and the stained glass windows smashed. When the members of the congregation saw the damage they marvelled at the sight that greeted them, as although the church appeared devastated, the magnificent church organ survived and still played. The hymn 'Now thank we all our God' was sung in appreciation of this miracle. The church was unable to be used for three months and during this time the services were held in the church hall until the church could be repaired. In Easter, 1944, worship was able to be resumed in the main church, but all the stained glass windows were bricked up and would so remain until their restoration in 1949, when they were rebuilt in the same style as the stained glass windows of St George's Church in Crowstone Road.

Avenue Road Baptist Church still stands today with an active congregation.

Baptist church interior, prior to 1920

ST GEORGE'S PRESBYTERIAN CHURCH

The site for St George's was purchased by Henry Robson for £600 on 14th July, 1896. A tent was erected on the site for the first service which was held on the following Sunday by the Rev R C Gillie, M.A. In October of the same year Southend was recognised by the Presbytery as a 'preaching station' and the Rev Davis Fotheringham was appointed as its Moderator. The tent was badly damaged by stormy weather and on at least one occasion the service was held with the Preacher having to lead the congregation from under an umbrella. A severe gale finally destroyed what was left of the tent and services were temporarily held at the Westcliff Hotel until more permanent premises were found.

In 1897 St George's Presbyterian Church was built on the Park Road site by the builders, Davis and Leavy of Colchester and Southend. It was designed by the architect Thomas Arnold, F.R.I.B.A., and, when completed, cost £6,112. The foundation stone was laid by the railway engineer, Sir George Bruce. It was a typical late Victorian red brick building with a tower on one corner and a church hall at the rear. On the 25th March, 1898, the new building was opened and the service was officiated by the Rev John Watson. Admission was by ticket with 200 seats being reserved for members and friends. Despite the snow and extreme snow that winter the church was crowded. Dr Watson conducted the service during a severe gale which at times made his voice scarcely audible.

The church membership built up from the from the first membership in May, 1897, of 29 names to a healthy congregation. Sir Henry Robson laid the foundation stone of the church hall on 22nd July, 1898. Unfortunately, there was difficulties with the heating system, which continually smoked; on one occasion there was so much smoke in the hall that the service had to be abandoned.

In 1980, because of falling congregations the church was closed and amalgamated with Crowstone United Reformed Church in Kings Road, Westcliff, which from then on was known as Crowstone St George's United Reformed Church.

In March, 1983, the site and the redundant church were purchased by the Abbeyfield Southend East Essex Society for £95,000 for the building of an Abbeyfield Extra Care House, an old peoples' home. Demolition took place between May and July of that year. A 20 resident extra care house for the frail and elderly was built on the site for a cost of £560,000 for the building and a further £75,000 for the furniture and equipment. The new building was named Abbeyfield St George's House to commemorate the old church.

When the church was demolished a 'time capsule' was found, consisting of a glass jar about 9 inches tall and 6 inches in diameter, buried beneath the original foundation stone of 1897. It contained a letter signed by the Moderator, the Chaplain of the local Committee and the Church Secretary, describing the origins of the church, a copy of *The Presbyterian*, visiting cards from the clergymen present at the ceremony and the original copy of the minutes of the Home Mission Committee of the Presbyterian Church in London approving a grant of £5,070 towards the cost of the building. There was also a copy of the *Southend Standard* of 22nd July, 1897, and a medallion celebrating Queen Victoria's Jubilee, 1897, showing Prime Ministers during her reign.

On 2nd August, 1985, under the foundation stone of the new Abbeyfield St George's House, there has been buried a new 'time capsule'. It contains a short history of the site, photographs of the original foundation stone, extracts from minutes of the Home Mission Committee of the Presbyterian Church, dated 18th November, 1895, report on St George's Church, dated 22nd July, 1897, photographs of St George's Church before demolition, demolition of St George's Church in progress, photographs of Brian Powell (architect of the new building) recovering the time capsule in May, 1983, leaflets *What is Abbeyfield?* and *The Abbeyfield St George's Extra Care Appeal*, programme for the laying of the foundation stone of the new building on 2nd August, 1988, copy of *Newsletter* No.1 of 'The Friends of Abbeyfield St George's', extracts from *Essex Countryside* magazine issues of August, 1983, September, 1986, April, 1985, two letter cards with photographs of Southend 1985, prizewinning letter from Bayswater High School (Australia) with suggestions for items to be included in the time capsule and a set of current coins lp to £1.

Hamlet Court Road, showing Coronation decorations, 23rd May, 1937 *(reproduced by permission of the Essex Record Office)*

ST HELEN'S ROMAN CATHOLIC CHURCH AND SCHOOL

The first mass to be held at Our Lady St Helen's Church was on 26th October, 1869. Previously, the Catholic congregation of Southend held their services in the upper room of Father John Moore's house at 3 Capel Terrace. Father Moore was educated in Paris and Rome and was 56 when he came to Southend in 1862 to be Southend's Catholic priest for 28 years. A kind man with genial manners, every Sunday he walked from Capel Terrace to Shoebury Garrison to say Mass for the troops before returning to Southend to say Mass for the Southend Catholics in the converted chapel at his house.

Father Moore worked hard in raising money to get St Helen's built and many leading Protestants contributed to his funds, but the church was mainly built through the generosity of Countess Helen Tasker of Middleton Hall, Brentwood. In 1867 tenders were invited for the building of the church under Mr W J Goodman, who was the architect. Seven firms replied, their tenders were as follows:

Brown and Robinson	£2,157
Axford	£2,125
Teacap	£2,100
Wicks, Bangs and Co.	£1,790
Wheeler	£1,770
Partman	£1,754
Wilkins and Son	£1,700

Wilkins and Son's tender was accepted and St Helen's was built for £1,700. The Archbishop of Westminster opened the church on 26th October, 1869. Philip Benton describes the church in his book *The History of Rochford Hundred* as:

In its design he [the architect] has aimed at producing an union of brick and stone at once pleasing, economical and effective... The nave measures 62 feet in the clear, by 21½ feet. the turret contains two bells from the foundry of Messrs. Mears and Stainbank, and its height is equal to the beautiful tower of the parish church. It is crowned by and angel vane, fully gilt, with lily in hand as the Angel of the Annunciation. The style of the Church is early English.

St Helen's Roman Catholic School was built later. In 1923/24 the average number of children on the school's register was 235, with the average attendance of 207 children, two of whom gained scholarships, one to St Bernard's Convent School and one to the Boys' High School. By 1937 the school had expanded to 309 children aged between 5-15 years old in seven classes. The School Inspector commenting in his report of that year said: 'There is a hard working headmaster and seven woman teachers and an excellent spirit in the school.'

St Bernard's Convent was in a building called the Mitre Hotel - more of a pub than an hotel. In the house there is still the remains of a beer cellar, complete with shute leading from the cellar to the corner on the ground floor. This convent must be one of few to have the remains of a room especially designed to hold alcohol.

Our Lady & St Helen's, Westcliff on Sea

Lady Chapel, Our Lady & St Helen's

In St Bernard's School there survives a unique reminder of the dwelling's earlier history - a store cupboard marked 'the Poor Man's Room'. When still a convent the Poor Man's Room was where the nuns fed the local vagrants, some of whom could be violent. The door to the room had a primitive electric automatic door, which could only be opened by pressing a button. The nuns dispensed food from behind a door with a glass panel enabling them to view the beggar, thus ensuring the protection of the holy sisters and the convent as a whole.

There is also a special door in St Bernard's called the Priests' Door. The priests lived in a home in Hermitage Road, at the back of the convent, called St Dominic's: they would enter the religious house by their own special portal, the Priests' Door, which still can be seen in the building, painted blue.

When the convent started there was not much money, so the nuns had to be self-sufficient. For this purpose a farmyard with chickens and pigs to supplement the holy sisters' meagre diet, was created at the back of the premises.

St Bernard's School arose from the work of the nuns of the convent. The nunnery had been an orphanage; these children needed an education, so a school was opened to provide for this need. Gradually the school grew and the nuns decided to expand. The facilities of the school were offered to children of the outside world. Thus the school grew from the seeds of the convent. Today it is still a thriving school, although no longer run directly by the Bernardine sisters.

The educational standard was high as the Head Teacher commented in her report of 19th November, 1935: 'Nearly all children who were eligible to leave school during the year were all placed in good and suitable positions. As a rule the children remain at school until they obtain situations, thus avoiding the break between school and obtaining employment.'

St Helen's Church, School and Presbytery were badly damaged in the bombing raid of Southend on the night of 12th December, 1943, when 2,000 kilograms of bombs fell on the town. The octogenarian Canon of St Helen's, Patrick McKenna, and a visiting priest were having their supper at the time in the Presbytery when the bomb fell and the presbytery ceiling fell on them. Miraculously, they were not seriously injured.

Also damaged was the St Bernard's Convent and High School. A number of girls were trapped inside the Convent during the raid, who were rescued by the nuns and some soldiers who scrabbled to get them free. One nun was severely injured in the blast, but twenty children who were boarders were led to safety by the nuns.

In 1970 St Helens celebrated its centenary. The *Southend Standard* marked the event and in 4th June, 1970, the following appeared:
'Next Wednesday, the Bishop of Brentwood will celebrate the Centenary Mass at St Helen's and afterwards preside at a dinner at the Kursaal Ballroom. Special guest will be the Bishop of Lancaster, Rt Rev Brian Falet.'

St Helen's Roman Catholic Church still stands, but St Helen's Roman Catholic School has new premises in North Road, Southend.

London Road, Westcliff, 31st May, 1927 (*reproduced by permission of the Essex Record Office*)

London Road, looking west from North Road, 12th June, 1924 Williams & Howard on left:
J Leeson on right (*reproduced by permission of the Essex Record Office*)

TWENTIETH CENTURY MILTON

MILTON ROAD - PARK ROAD

At the beginning of the 20th century Milton had shrunk to what was known as the Park Estate, named after Southend Park, which once stood there. The estate stretched from Park Road to Milton Road and consisted of a wide variety of different styles of houses and shops.

There was a small parade of shops at one end of Park Road. No 2 Park Road, the shop on the corner, was a greengrocers and fruiterers always referred to as 'Arnold's'. Mr and Mrs Arnold were a very kind couple with a reputation for spoiling all the local children of the neighbourhood. One local resident, Mrs Keen, recalling her childhood spent in Avenue Road in the early years of this century, remembers:

'I benefited (from the Arnold's kindness) when recovering from some childhood illness I was ordered by the doctor to have an orange a day. Each morning without fail Mrs. Arnold sent 'the boy' to our back door, or came herself, to deliver my special orange!'

Next door to Arnold's, at No. 4 Park Road, was Mrs Dowsett's sweet shop, where even if you had only a ha'penny or perhaps even less, only a farthing to spend, Mrs Dowsett or her assistant, Elsie, would fold a small paper into a cone and fill it with goodies like liquorice all-sorts, fruit drops, or jellies. French almond rock or chocolate were treats as any quantity of these required at least sixpence. Mrs Dowsett was a niece of Mr Thomas Dowsett, the first Mayor of the Borough of Southend.

No 6 Park Road was a milliners owned by two sisters. It was indeed a milliners, not merely a hat shop. Hats were made or trimmed to suit one's own style or taste. Mrs Keen recalls the shop:

'I remember however being very disappointed when I asked for a bunch of artificial cherries as trimming for a new winter velour hat and was refused, very politely but firmly of the grounds that 'it would not suit you, dear'. Aged seven, I was not a very satisfied customer, but had to submit to the powers that be!'

No 8 Park Road was the newsagents, stationers, and sub-post office, and was a very busy shop. The owner's name was Everitt, but in the nineteen twenties the shop was taken over by the Abbott family. Mr R A Abbott was postmaster for many years and, when he retired, his son continued the shop until his retirement in the nineteen seventies, when the sub-post office closed and the shop became a general stores.

No 10 Park Road was the only private house in the small parade and the only one with a small front garden. It was owned by the Methodists and occupied by the Caretaker of Park Road Methodist Church situated directly opposite. The house was converted into a shop in 1968.

No 12 Park Road was a grocers owned by Mr W H Cullen. It was again a high-class shop and one where you could leave a weekly order, which would be delivered. There were no difficulties about carrying heavy shopping in those days!

London Road, looking west from Victoria Circus, 14th November, 1919 (*reproduced by permission of the Essex Record Office*)

London Road, looking west from Princes Street (*reproduced by permission of the Essex Record Office*)

Across the road at No 1 Park Road, near the railway bridge, was a barber's. It had a red and white sugar stick coloured pole outside and a signboard which advertised hairdressing to ladies and children. Mrs Keen has vivid memories of having her long, straight, unmanageable hair trimmed and singed at the ends there, so much so that burnt hair always reminded her of the Park Road barbershop.

At the other end of that parade was a small haberdasher's selling buttons, ribbon, elastic, etc. This shop was very handy if you couldn't find replenishments in your work box to repair a broken knicker elastic or replace a lost hair ribbon.

The remains of the old mill were still to be seen at the back of that small parade of shops by the railway bridge. Some of the old buildings at the rear of Shelford House, which were used as stables, were said to be the mill out-buildings. The mill, which was demolished in about 1892, left a site on which all the local children played.

Shelford House was a noted building of the area belonging to the Belcham family. In the outbuildings attached to the house sheep were kept temporarily from the Belcham Farm for subsequent delivery to their slaughterhouse behind Gordon Belcham's butcher shop on the corner of Park Street and Hamlet Road.

At No 84 Hamlet Road, just round the corner from Park Road, Samuel Taylor traded as Taylor the Bootmakers. A showcase displaying the latest styles in ladies' and gents' boots and shoes stood across the entrance to the shop and was backed by mirrors. When the shop door was open, which it was invariably, these mirrors reflected the bright green hawthorn hedge flanking the London, Tilbury and Southend Railway line opposite. This hedge was quite thick and a good height and on those occasions when the sheep were being moved any passer-by looking into those mirrors would have been forgiven for thinking he was in a country lane. Mrs Keen recalls:
'On this day my father was working quietly in his office at the rear of the shop when he was startled by a tremendous noise. He looked up from his work to see a sheep emerge from the showcase having broken through the clear glass, forced open the mirror doors scattering boots, shoes, and glass in the process. Before father could recover from the shock, the sheep rushed through the showroom, through the back entrance door, fortunately open, and out in the back yard where it collapsed, terribly injured and subsequently had to be destroyed.'

By the 1930's the area around Milton Road was self-sufficient in shops, having many varied businesses. In *Kelly's Directory* of 1931, Park Road was listed as having a confectioner, drapers, stationers, and general stores. Milton Road had a large variety of different shops and businesses: solicitor, two milliners, two hairdressers, chemist, watch-maker, drapers, a cretonne shop (which stocked the popular patterned fabric used for upholstery, frocks, etc.) two decorators, chimney sweep, Westcliff Removal Company, two greengrocers, stationer, oilman, fishmonger, second-hand furniture shop, dining rooms, butcher, tailor, costumier, Woodyatt Motors, cycle agents, wardrobe dealer, grocer, baker, coal merchants, two confectioners, Exide battery depôt, a plumber, and a public house.

Junction of Park Street and Queen's Road, 25th September, 1928 (*reproduced by permission of the Essex Record Office*)

Hamlet Court Road, 2nd November, 1907 (*reproduced by permission of the Essex Record Office*)

All this in one street, truly a cornucopia of shopping!

In Milton Road the fish and chip shop which sold both wet and dry fish was noted for its quality of produce, as was the butchers for its sausages, said to be the best in town. There were always queues outside these shops as their reputation for fine food grew. The drapers, called Knights, was a large double fronted shop which sold material and artificial flowers for hats. Local children would earn much appreciated pocket money by collecting clean newspapers and bottles on the cliffs for use by the fish-mongers. They also used to clean the drains, which frequently overflowed after heavy rainfall, flooding the road by the drapers.

Milton Road was a hive of activity in pre-war days. The Cricketers Inn, so called after cricket fields opposite the inn before the Park Estate was built, was the centre of the local community and weekend dances were held in its hall, which was alongside.

Mr William Heddle, a notable resident, lived in Park Road. He was Bishop of the Peculiar People Church. The Peculiar People derived their name from a quotation from the Bible. They were a very strict Christian group who, among other things, did not believe in medical care and refused to have operations, preferring to leave things to God's care. Some members served prison sentences for refusing medical attention for their children.

William founded the local drapery shop of Heddles, which was a large shop situated in Park Street. Over the years it built up a good reputation for personal service and was one of the premier drapers in the town. After a long and distinguished trading career the shop finally closed its doors in the late nineteen seventies. The business was started when he strapped parcels of merchandise to his chest and back, laboriously treading the Essex roads to hawk his wares.

Bishop Heddle joined the Peculiar People in 1873. Disagreement arose in the sect about what degree of medical treatment was allowed. A split took place, the Peculiar People being led by Bishop Heddle and Elder Chigrell, who stuck to the principles of the movement, and an opposing faction called the Original Peculiar People led by George Harrod and James Anderson. In 1911 and 1912 steps were taken to end this split and a meeting was called where Heddle and Chigrell confronted Harrod and Anderson. To the relief of all concerned, the opposing sides reached an agreement over a cup of tea at the meeting and spent the evening amicably together. A grand reunion meeting was arranged to celebrate at Southend on New Year's Day, 1913, and a record number of Peculiar People attended.

Bishop Heddle retired from active duties in the church in 1942. In 1946 he celebrated his 100th birthday, having lived to Peculiar People principles ever since his conversion in 1873. No doctor had ever been called to attend him, he had taken no pills or any medical prescriptions or ever eaten a cooked meal on a Sunday. He died two years later in 1948, deeply mourned by his fellow church members.

In Milton Road was the town's first waterworks. Run by a private company founded in 1865, the water pumping station served a population of 1,700 residents in

Bomb damage at St Bernard's (*reproduced by permission of the Essex Record Office*)

St Vincent's bomb damage (*reproduced by permission of the Essex Record Office*)

what was then known as Cliff Town, and daily pumped out 1,600 gallons of water, about one gallon per person. Later a further reservoir was built in Cambridge Road which was still in use up to the late nineteen eighties, when the land was finally used for further housing. In 1871, the waterworks was taken over by the Southend Waterworks Co. Ltd.

One of the largest houses in the Park Estate was Barons Court, a private house with its entrance in Avenue Road. For a short period it was a school before becoming Barons Hotel, a noted hotel of the area with its own private tennis courts in the grounds. During the Second World War the army requisitioned it, only to let the building fall into disrepair. It was pulled down in 1948, about eighteen months after the end of the war. The land was temporarily distributed as allotments. In 1968 a school was built on the site, taking as its name Barons Court Infants' School, after the old building.

St Bernard's Convent in Milton Road was originally a hotel named the Mitre. On the 7th July, 1870, it first opened its doors as a convent, then called St Mary's Convent. The convent was first run by the Sisters of Nôtre Dame, a German Order. An orphanage certified for fifty children was opened by the nuns on 13th December, 1879, and a day school followed on the 3rd December, 1889. The nuns of the Order were buried in the church yard in the Convent grounds. The bitter fighting and general hardships of the First World War generated an intense dislike of Germans who lived in this country, so the nuns left the convent and returned to Germany. The building was taken over by the 'Religious Bernardines', a French Order, and in 1918 renamed St Bernard's Convent. The Bernardines continued the work of the convent and school, now called St Bernard's School.

St Vincent's Road, developed from the Vincent's Farm in 1874, was built as a high class road backing on to the Southend Park. The large houses were sold to families with a full staff of servants. Southend Park became a favourite place for the nannies of these families to walk their charges in their prams. Signs saying 'No hawkers, no circulars' were firmly fixed to the gates of these houses. Later some very exclusive private schools sprung up in the road.

St Vincent's Road was involved in the Zeppelin attack of May, 1915, on the town. A bomb actually landed in the street itself, though luckily no one was injured. The *Southend and Westcliff Graphic* of Tuesday, 11th May, 1915, ran a special Zeppelin supplement reporting the incident, stating:

'At five minutes to three yesterday [Monday] morning, Southend was startled by two terrific explosions and almost simultaneously the sky was lit up by flames in different parts of the Borough. When the airship was seen, her glow in the sky could be seen and she was using a searchlight. A warning was sounded by the town hooter, the signal for people to remain in their houses, but hundreds ran into the streets to have a sight of her. There was no panic.'

Avenue Road is one of the oldest streets in the Borough, once having been the main

Palmeira Arches under construction (*reproduced by permission of the Essex Record Office*)

Milton Road (*reproduced by permission of the Essex Record Office*)

road running to Hamlet Mill in Park Road. It contains an oddity; it has two Number Thirteens. The first is on the south side and is the last house in that stretch of Avenue Road: its neighbour is 1, St Vincent's Road. On the opposite side is also No. 13 Avenue Road, the house marked 13a, part of a terrace built by Topsfield, the builder who resided in the street.

The Park Estate had many prominent local business people living there, including the Heddle family, the Jacksons and the Sopers.

MILTON CONSERVATION AREA

By the early 20th century, the historical name of Milton was being subsumed, merged into the new Borough of Southend and Westcliff. Only a few reminders were left, an old street name, an old name of a building.

A small proportion of the original Milton was designated by Southend Borough Council into the Milton Conservation Area. This area stretches between Park Road and Milton Road and between London Road and Southend-Fenchurch Street railway line. It is in these roads that the Doomsday name of Milton lives on, although in a much reduced state.

Councillor J Wade described the area in the foreword of *The Milton Conservation Guide* as:

'We are fortunate in possessing areas of historic and architectural importance such as Milton, which give Southend its unique character and which, in turn, enhance our sense of community and encourage us to set high standards for development and redevelopment in the town.'

The houses in this area of the town, known as the Park Estate, named after Southend Park, which was situated there, show a rich variance of architectural style. Milton has kept its Victorian and Edwardian character.

Milton, the foundation of Southend and Westcliff, has now faded from the town's memory. Perhaps it is now time to look back and remember the true source of the Borough of Southend and of Westcliff on Sea and give it the recognition it deserves.

Cricketers' Corner
(reproduced by permission of the Essex Record Office)

CHALKWELL AND THE CROWSTONE

Chalkwell was a part of that large but forgotten part of the town, Milton. The manor of Chalkwell is mentioned in the will of Robert Swete, the tenant in 1493. During this period it was held as part of what was known as the "Knight's Fee" of Milton.

This was an obligation in feudal days for the tenant to provide a fully armed and equipped knight together with retainers for military service to the crown. For tenure of the land Robert Swete paid an annual sum of rent of 23s.3d, this included his knight's service and three of the best living creatures for heriots, which were the finest beasts a manor could provide. When Robert Swete died he left instructions in his will that he was to be buried next to his parents at St Mary's in Prittlewell and at his funeral three sheep were to be driven to the church before his body. Swete was a rich man, he owned over 300 sheep on Foulness and these three animals were an offering to the church.

The name Chalkwell is strange as there is there is no chalk in the soil. But there was an old well in the grounds of Chalkwell Hall. One of its tenants, Soloman Monk, who resided there between 1782-1826 installed a spring pump there. The local historian Benton mentions a spring to the west of the manor house from which there was a well about six feet deep. But there is no trace of it now. Perhaps it was originally lined with chalk.

Chalkwell was originally a settlement of farmers and agricultural labourers with perhaps a few oyster fishermen. When the railway to Southend was constructed in 1854, particular provisions had to be made for Chalkwell. An empowering Act specially required two level-crossings and a siding to be made at Chalkwell for the use of the farm. Although the region began to be developed in 1900-1910, the area was so rural that there were fields between Chalkwell Park and the railway up to the 1930s.

Chalkwell Park houses the manor house of Chalkwell, Chalkwell Hall. This building was erected in 1830, the previous building being demolished in 1832. The present building is the third house on the site. The first dwelling stood in a field called Moat field near the railway. Traces of this fortified house remained until 1867.

There are magnificent wrought iron gates at the entrance to the park. These were given to the town by Mr Percy Raven in memory of his son, Warrant Officer Eric Raven. The Raven family are noted Southend traders and still have a well-known store in Cliff Town Road. The business was built up by Percy Raven who in 1939 gave his recipe for success in the local paper, *The Southend Standard*:

"First make up your mind and decide what you want. That is the main point. Then get down to it. Whatever you have chosen as a career, go all out for, and do not be persuaded from your course. It is the vision and the will to achieve it that is the secret of success."

Excellent advice that still holds true.

The splendid grounds of Chalkwell Park itself houses a memorial Garden of

Remembrance to commemorate the fallen of the Second World War. This beautiful park was purchased for Southend Corporation in 1901 for approximately £20,000.

There was drama in the park in 1934, when an unexploded First World War bomb was found. It was spotted by Mr Stebbin, who was engaged in returning the pitch of the Leigh Cricket Club. When the shocked man dug his fork in the ground, the prongs touched a metal object, thinking it was a metal pipe, Mr Stebbin was horrified to find that object was in fact a bomb. The bomb was 2ft 6ins in length and five to six inches in diameter. As the *Southend Standard* put it: "The circumstances makes Mr Stebbin very thankful that he was not using a pick at the time." The bomb was very carefully carried to the Park hut and from there to the Westcliff Police Station, where it was presumably made safe.

The Chalkwell Hall estate was highly desirable when built. The estate covered an area of 262 acres and included Chalkwell Park. Eighteen houses were constructed in 1902. By 1915, the number of houses on the estate had risen to 287.

Perhaps today most people would associate Chalkwell with the sea front. Westcliff and Chalkwell Esplanades were constructed in 1903 for the large sum in those days of £42,000. The walk was extended into Southend to the Pier in 1914 for a further £100,000. It along this parade in Chalkwell that there are some unusual cafés. These remarkable eateries are constructed from splendid brick archways. There were other arches, at the foot of Shorefield Gardens. These red brick arches were originally summer chalets, which families rented from a local estate agent for an annual payment of £12 to £22. They provided comfortable accommodation with oil fuelled lighting, heating and ovens for cooking. One of the tenants, Mr Fisher, gives a vivid description of the inside of one of the chalets that his family had inhabited in 1919 in the *Southend Standard* of 17th September, 1970:

"They were summer chalets "with thick coconut matting on the floors, attractive wicker chairs and matching glass-topped tables and a small dresser."

They sound very comfortable. Mr Fisher continues to describe the spectacular view that there was over the Estuary:

"We had an unobstructed view across the river and I can well remember the wonderful sight of the Fleet assembled in the Thames for the victory celebrations after the First World War."

These unusual buildings were used as ammunition dumps for troops in the Second World War who occupied the terrace of houses in Shorefield Gardens. They then fell into disuse.

In a magnificent position above the cliffs lies the West Cliff Hotel, which has an interesting history. At the turn of the century Southend had a strong temperance movement and the drinking of alcohol was strictly frowned on. The town was developing fast and there was a need for good hotels. The West Cliff was built, but was erected as a temperance hotel, where no alcoholic drinks were allowed.

The town already had a Temperance Hotel. In 1878 the *Southend Standard*

Westcliff Esplanade under construction, 1904
Overcliff Hotel and Parade

contained an advertisement for the Southend Temperance Institute in Alexandra Street. The name of this building was changed to the Victoria Temperance Hotel and Coffee Palace in 1892. The original Institute composed of a reading room with books, magazines and daily newspapers. When the site was expanded and became the Victoria it now consisted of enough room for 700 people to sit down for "bean-feasts", which were annual dinner given by employers to their workers and a general time of merriment. Though presumably this was without any alcoholic refreshment, the enjoyment might have been limited. Now guests could stay at this establishment for 1s.6d. per night inclusive.

In 1891 the West Cliff Hotel was built, the second temperance building in the town. It was a luxurious building the only hotel in the area that had four baths. The opening was an important event. It is recorded in July 1891, by the *Southend Standard*:

"The hotel is a handsome and well proportioned building five storeys high, built in the decorative classic style. It has a frontal to West Cliff and slopping cliffs in front have been acquired by Mr. Stubbs so that patrons will have a fine and uninterrupted view of the sea; this ground will shortly be laid out as pleasure grounds for those using the hotel".

Mr William Stubbs, a successful carter and barge owner in London, was the owner and visionary who conceived the hotel, but it was beset by rumours. It was said that the title 'temperance' was only temporary, and that the hotel would soon be licensed. The gossip reached the local paper. In the "A look round" section of the newspaper this tittle-tattle was firmly scotched: "Rumour is once more in error," the writer wrote, "for Mr Stubbs is a great man among Good Templars, and combines serious philanthropic intent with business resource and push."

Mr. Stubbs was very pleased with the new hotel. A lover of the town, he saw the potential of this enterprise. He could see good lucrative commercial possibilities:

"We have within 50 miles or this little town," he said, "a population concentrated and settled equal, or more than equal to the whole of Scotland, or the whole of Ireland, to the whole of Sweden and Norway, or to the whole of Switzerland. What a harvest there is to be reaped from that vast population."

But the question of the status of alcohol at the West Cliff was again under dispute. At the application in August, 1891, for the erection of another hotel, the Hotel Metropole, which later became the Palace, magistrates heard that people were getting around the restrictions of the temperance movement. The solicitor for the applicants stated:

"Are you aware that visitors to the temperance hotel on the cliffs are bringing their own wine? And that last only last evening at the Temperance Hotel, visitors' own wine was upon the table being consumed? And that visitors decline to stay unless they are allowed to drink their own wine?"

You can imagine the shock and horror this statement caused to the Victorians at the hearing. In fact, a member of the Sons of Phoenix, a Temperance Friendly Society,

Stalls in Western Esplanade below Shorefields Pavilion, 10th July, 1925 (*reproduced by permission of the Essex Record Office*)

Cliffs at Westcliff, 14th December, 1911 (*reproduced by permission of the Essex Record Office*)

Mr W. G. Brighten, disapprovingly said: "We can't help it if a man opens a hotel on a professedly temperance principles, and then at the first blush of opposition turns tail and gives them up. Mr Stubbs is no member of our Order."

Despite all the opposition from the Sons of Phoenix and the West Cliff and Royal hotels, the magistrates did grant a provisional licence to the Metropole. It was the thin edge of the wedge. The Metropole was granted a full licence in 1896. The Queens and Grand hotels followed 1898 and 1899. But the West Cliff stuck to its temperance principles. It did not get a licence to sell alcoholic drink until 1923.

But possibly the town is best known for its mud. Southend and Westcliff's mud were thought to have healing properties. Over the years many schemes have been suggested to utilise these unusual resources.

A big fan of the curative properties of the mud was the vicar of St Johns, Rev J. J. Whitehouse. In the *Southend Observer* in 1943 he enthused about the remedial power of the mud. He said that it should be commercialised, and that the town could become a thriving spa.

This is not a new idea. In 1924, Mr Pam Biamco had a similar idea. Mr Biamco called himself a *'Dottore Profesore'* and gave a rather unusual and unlikely address of 'House of Commons, Rome', where ever that is. But he was very enthusiastic about Southend's mud. Giving his opinion: "I believe that your fango (fango is a clay or mud from thermal springs in Italy, and is used in the treatment of gout, rheumatism, etc.) is worth special interest and attention from the industrial point of view, more particularly as regards its medicinal use." He even claimed that he had the mud analyzed. A water based clinic was suggested capable of accommodating 50 patients a day. The cost of this building would be £1,100. Two sites were chosen in Benfleet.

Here it was thought that the: "mud, ferruginous peat, sea water, seaweed, and other saline plants - all of great therapeutic and exceptional quality can be secured within easy reach."

There was also another bizarre scheme utilising this precious asset. This was to use the "Radio Active Mud from the Southend and Westcliff foreshore for the purpose of extracting the radium elements contained therein, for the production of radio-active oil, embrocation, liniments, ointments, etc., curative properties of which have been fully established after many years of research work by the discoverer, and are the subject of patents." It does not say which patents are being referred to. But there was assurances of the marketing potential of the radio active oils and preparations that included face and massage creams, pills, cough mixtures, embrocations, hair tonics and brilliantine! No doubt these potions would have been effective, but the curative powers of radio active mud really does seem very weird.

In days gone by not everybody was law abiding. There were stories of smuggling. The *Southend Times* in 1928 gives a vivid description of the life of a smuggler as seen through the eyes of a ninety year old man looking back to his childhood. Mr James Moss gave a colourful account of his early years to the newspaper on his ninetieth birthday. Mr Moss, speaking from his Rayleigh home, described the antics of smugglers in the town in the middle of the nineteenth century, when he was just a young lad:

"My father was a great smuggler and he had to fly from the country to escape the Excise men. All his smuggler friends - mine too - were deported. I remember when boats used to creep up the river at night to Stambridge, loaded with tobacco and spirits. Father kept a bus, known as 'The Ghost Bus'. so called because, when the darkness fell, we used to bind the wheels of the bus with thick cloth and cover the horses' hoofs with heavy but soft sponge, to make them silent.

"Then the 'Ghost Bus' would glide softly and swiftly through the dark country lanes to the river to collect the smuggled goods from the boats.

"Strangely enough, though we had so much to do with spirits and tobacco, none of my family smoked and I am practically a teetotaller. Perhaps familiarity breeds contempt!

"Secret tunnels running underground used to be used by the smugglers, but they have now fallen in, or been closed. In 1850 a man called Peter Wright was one of the most daring smugglers of the day. Peter, with my father, one day hid some large bales of tobacco, under a huge mound of earth. Suddenly two Excise men rode up and one plunged a long spear into the mound. They pulled it out, smelt the end, detected the tobacco - and we were caught!"

It was certainly a more exciting life than that of today, although a lot more dangerous.

Life has changed a lot.

Holiday visitors start for a ride from
13a Avenue Road, Summer, 1907

Chalkwell Esplanade under construction, 24th October, 1903 *(reproduced by permission of the Essex Record Office)*

Chalkwell beach, 1904 *(reproduced by permission of the Essex Record Office)*

THE CROWSTONE

The most noticeable feature of Chalkwell is the Crowstone in the Thames Estuary. This stone marks the jurisdiction of the City of London's control of the River Thames. To the east of the Crowstone the estuary is in law the high sea. The eastern limit of the lawful authority of the City is earmarked by what is known as the London Stone, at the northern entrance to Yantlet Creek on the Isle of Grain. The original obelisk that was made of Portland stone was removed and re-erected at Upnor on the north bank of the Medway. A new stone was mounted in the water during the early part of the 19th century. The western limit of the City was marked by a stone erected at Staines and is called the City Stone. This latter stone is no longer a marker for the boundary that is now at Teddington, where a new stone was assembled to mark the spot.

Every so often these marker stones were replaced a new column being installed in its place. A replacement stone at Leigh was erected in 1755. Daniel Pinder, mason, was paid £46.11s.4d. for erecting two new boundary stones at Cookham Wood in the River Medway and at Lea (Leigh) in Essex in 1789. The records do not state whether this was payment for his work at Leigh in 1755, if so, it appears the poor man had to wait thirty-four years for reimbursement. But there is suggestive correspondence in the archives dated 15th December, 1789, which points to that:

"Chamberlain to pay Daniel Pinder, mason, £46.11.0d. "for providing and fixing two new boundary stones at Cookham Wood in the River Medway and at Leigh in Essex... by order of William Gill Esq., late Lord Mayor."

NB £46-11s-4d in City Cash Accounts for 1789."

I can find no evidence to suggests that there were any other stones erected at Chalkwell apart from that in 1755.

Daniel Pinder restored a number of the marker stones for the Corporation of the City of London. There is a document dated 22nd Oct 1782 authorising payment to the mason for work on the boundary stone at Staines:

"Chamberlain to pay Daniel Pinder mason £31.1s.0d. - "for erecting a pedestal and repairing the City's Boundary Stone at Staines ... by order of Sir Watkin Lewis Knight the Lord Mayor".

The work was carried out in the 1781, the year of Sir Watkin Lewis's mayoralty. The stone must have looked splendid on its new plinth.

The boundary stones were replaced regularly. Two new stones were erected at Upnor and Leigh in 1837 at what was then the astronomical sum of £205.1s.5d.: an awful lot of money. The records date this on the 17th October of that year: "caused Granite Boundary Stones on Pillars to be placed at Upnor near Rochester in the County of Kent and at Leigh near Southend in the County of Essex."

In both places the two stones remained, the older and smaller adjacent to the more modern and larger stone.

The control of the river was first given by Richard I in 1197 by a formal grant in return for a sum of 1,500 marks. This was a vast some of money, F S Thacker in his work *The Thames Highway*, published in 1914, assesses that this was worth £20,000, and that was in 1914! The value of 1,500 marks would now be considerably higher. This money was used by Richard to fund his Crusades.

Here is a translation of the 1197 Charter from Walter De Gray Birch *The Historical Charters & Constitutional Documents of the City of London*. The grants of jurisdiction were confirmed by stature, not charter in 1285. A charter being a deed or instrument in writing granted by the sovereign or Parliament, whereas a statute can only be granted by a legislative body. Here is the Charter:

THE SECOND CHARTER OF RICHARD
14th July AD 1197

Richard, by the grace of God, king of England, duke of Normandy, and earl of Anjou; To his archbishops,. Bishops, abbots, earls, barons, justices, sheriffs, stewards, castle-keepers, justices, constables, bailiffs, ministers, and all his faithful subjects, greeting.
Know ye all that we, for the health of our soul, and for the soul's health of our father, all our ancestors souls; and also for the common weal of our city of London, and of all our realm, have grantee and steadfastly commanded, that all ears that are in the Thames be removed, wheresoever they shall be with the Thames (and that no wears from hence for to be put anywhere in the Thames). Also we have quit-claimed all that which the keeper of our Tower of London was wont yearly to receive of the said wears. Wherefore we will and steadfastly command, that no keeper of the said Tower, at any time hereafter, shall exact any thing of any one, neither molest nor burden, nor any demand make of any person, by reason of the said wears. For it is manifest to us, and by our right reverend father, Hubert, archbishop of Canterbury [Hubert Walter], and other our faithful subjects, it is sufficiently given us to understand, that great detriment and discommodity bath grown to our said city of London and also to the whole realm, by occasion of the said wears. Which thing, to the intent it may continue for ever firm and stable, we do fortify by the inscription of this present page, and the putting to of our seal:

These being witnesses.
Hubert, archbishop of Canterbury; John of Worcester, Hugh of Coventry, bishops; John, earl of Moreton, Ralph, earl of Chester, Robert, earl of Leicester, William, earl of Arundel, earl William Marshall, William of St Mary's Church, Peter son of Herbert, Matthew his brother, Simon de Kyma, Seher de Quincy. Given by the hand of Eustace, dean of Salisbury, vice-chancellor, at the isle of Andely, on the fourteenth day of July, in the eighth year of our reign.

Altogether five separate charters were granted to the City for a total payment of 3,000 marks. The Charter of King John gave the citizens the jurisdiction to remove all the weirs in the Thames and Medway. It was almost word for word the same as the previous document but it added the authority to fine anyone breaking this law £10.

This charter was dated the 17th June, 1199. It was confirmed in the Magna Charta of 1215. This edict was so important that it was further confirmed by a Charter granted by Henry III on 18th February, 1277. But perhaps the most significant stature was that of Edward I in 1285. This stated that the Lord Mayor should have the conservancy of the Thames from Staines Bridge to London and in the Medway. It is this date that appears on the mark stones at Staines and Chalkwell.

These statutes were clearly to assist navigation on the river. Roger Griffiths in an essay in 1746 describes a case occurring in 1237 when these laws were breached:

"Jordan Coventry, one of the Sheriffs of London, was by the Mayor and Alderman sent to remove certain kiddells (kiddells or kiddles were screens of stakes or hurdles, thickly interwoven with twigs or brushwoods set in a tideway for catching fish) that annoyed the River of Thames and Medway: who ULTRA YENLAND VERSES MARE, did take divers persons that were offenders, and did Imprison them; whereupon complaint being made to King Henry Ill, who upon hearing of the said Matter, before the said King Henry, the City's jurisdiction was set forth and allowed, and the complainants convicted and every of them at £10 and the amercements (fines) adjudged to the City; and their nets were afterwards burned by Judgement, given to the Lord Mayor and Aldermen in the Hustings."

These kiddles trapped many immature fish, therefore ruining the fishing for legitimate fishermen. It was obviously a serious crime, if the sentence could include imprisonment. The burning of the nets would also have been a severe loss to the destitute fisherman.

The ban of the building of weirs continued throughout the fifteenth century. When Edward IV (1442-83) granted the Earl of Pembroke permission to construct a 'wear" in the Thames, it was bitterly contested by the Lord Mayor and Aldermen of the City. The City won their case as it was considered an encroachment on the ancient liberties. This is interesting as it shows that the City had more power than the Crown.

The preservation of fish was the prime aim and responsibility of the City. The building of weirs and anything that would destroy fish or fry were taken very seriously. The size of nets were strictly controlled. The guardianship and protection of the fish stocks were of overriding importance. There are several mediæval records stressing this fact. But gradually the emphasis passed to the improvement of inland navigation, as the amount of boats on the water increased. In 1770 the Corporation appointed a Navigation Committee to oversee the flow of traffic on the river. This became one of the City's busiest committees.

Navigation gradually took precedence over the preservation of fish stocks. The Water Bailiff, Roger Griffiths, writing in 1746, quotes an order which enacted that

"Timbers that lie floating and adrift on the River to the prejudice of either the Navigation or the Fishery... are seizable by the Water Bailiff. Griffiths continues, "Some annoying timbers in Tilbury Hope, below Gravesend, dangerous to passengers and to fishermen's nets were...by the pains and diligence of the Water Bailiff, all taken up and conveyed to Guildhall in London." Of course Griffiths was the Water Bailiff and his claim of "pain and diligence" would he hoped by noted by those in the relevant position in authority.

The area of jurisdiction of the Corporation until 1857 extended from the River Colne near Staines to Yantlett Creek, and included parts of the Rivers Medway and Lea, and all streams and creeks of tidal water within those bounds. A vast area.

The responsibility of the river was the Corporation of London until the Thames Conservancy Act of 1857 gave their powers to the Thames Conservators which were then transferred to the Port of London Authority by the Port of London Act, 1908. By 1908 the cost of dredging and the upkeep of the Thames to keep the flow of traffic on the river was very high. The total expenditure by this time was around £2,500,000 - a great deal of money. It is likely that the Thames Conservators were only too happy to pass all this to the Port of London Authority. But the health of the Port and of the ships using it remained the responsibility of the City Corporation. Today the launches of the Port Health Authority carry doctors to check the health of the crews of inward-bound ships in Gravesend Reach. This vital check for illness stops the spread of what could be fatal infectious plagues and diseases starting in the country.

There were two stones that used to stand in the Thames opposite Chalkwell Avenue, one large made of granite and the shorter of Portland Stone. The smaller pillar is square and just over seven feet high and is the original stone, is engraved with the names of former Lord Mayors of the City of London. In 1838, the larger obelisk 14 feet high was erected next to the archetypal construction. The smaller and older stone was completely covered with the names of the Lord Mayors and the new stone provided more room for further inscriptions.

Why these stones were called the Crowstone is a mystery. There is a local legend that they mark the spot where King Canute (c.994-1035) sat in his stately throne and told the sea to recede, and not to wet him. The tide of course continued to advance as the sea always has and Canute was drenched with foam. The king was said to have stated: "Let all the world know that the power of monarchs is vain ... no one deserves the name of King but He whose Will the Heavens, Earth and Sea do obey." Although a nice story, it is unlikely that the event described happened here in Essex, even though this part of Essex is connected with King Canute. Ashingdon is said to mark the Battle of Assandun where Canute defeated Edmund Ironside, (c.989-1016), the King of Wessex. Edmund led the resistance to Danish Canute's invasion of 1015, and, on Ethelred's death 1016, was chosen king by the citizens of London, whereas the Witan (the king's council) elected Canute. In the eventual struggle for the throne, Edmund was defeated by Canute at Assandun (Ashington), Essex, and they divided the kingdom between them. When Edmund died 1016 Canute ruled the whole kingdom and was crowned in 1017.

St Andrew's church in Ashingdon was said to have been founded by King Canute to mark his victory, the battle being fought on the hill on which the church stands. There is a legend that says that no grass would grow on the bloodstained hill. This hill and church were the site of pilgrimage. There was a shrine in the building at which miracles occurred. Pilgrims would crawl up the hill on the their knees to receive the blessings of the saint. This was a place where barren women went anxious to be fertile and give birth. It is still a church where it is considered very lucky to get married in. The couple will be blessed.

However, the above suggestion of the origin and reason for the Crowstone to be placed and named the actual intention is more mundane. The stones, are just a markstone for the boundary's of the City of London, but the name still intrigues.

W B Wyatt gave some suggestions in a paper he wrote for Southend-on-Sea Antiquarian and Historical Society in 1935:

"(a) A course gannister known locally as crowstone is quarried in parts of Derbyshire and Yorkshire, bit it is highly improbable that the stone at Leigh was obtained either of these localities.

(b) "Crow stone," "crow steps," or "corbie steps" are terms which occur in architectural nomenclature.

(c) Crowstone as a corruption of "cross stone" denoting the existence of a cross or stone marking the beginning of a hard crossing to Canvey.

(d) The stone as a resting place for the crows which abounded in the district.

Dr P H Reaney in his *Place Names of Essex*, says that there was a dwelling known as Crows in 1535, and that the stone was named Crowe's Stone after this site.

The debate on the origins of name Crowstone was still going on in 1951. There is a letter of that year from the Port of London Authority to the then Deputy Keeper of the Records. It gives five similar alternatives:

1. From being due north "as the crow flies" of the boundary stone at Yantlet Creek
2. From a type of stone known in Derbyshire and Yorkshire as "crowstone".
3. As a resting place of crows
4. From the architectural term "crow steps" (this is step-like stonework on a gable).
5. As a corruption of "Cross Stone" (e.g. are chiastolite; staurolite; harmotome, types of crystals, minerals and stones).

It is a mystery that will continue to fascinate local historians. But I suppose that the origin of this unusual name will be forever an enigma.

THE SMALLER STONE

On the smaller stone the appears the coat of arms of the City of London. There is also the date of 1285 written in Arabic numerals. This is the date that Edward I granted the powers and rights of the jurisdiction of the Thames to the City of London. But this is very strange as Arabic numerals for recording dates were very rare before the 15th century. This suggests that the stone was erected later than 1285. There had been marker stones at Leigh in the Thames stretching back for many years. The City Walter Bailiff, Roger Griffiths writing in 1746, describes the region and mentions that had been a Mark Stone in the area:

"A little below Canvey or rather opposite to the lower end of it, is a small town called Leigh, of little or no account, otherwise than it is well stocked with fishermen and seamen, and likewise that about two miles bellow this town the jurisdiction of London on the Essex side of the river terminates a place called Crow Stone, but by some accident it has been lost these several years past."

There is a dramatic document dating the important ceremony in 1755 which replaced an earlier stone.

It gives a fascinating account of the ritual involved. Here is an extract from the Reportary of the describing procedure of the erection of the Crowstone on the 25th August, 1755:

"On Monday the 25th August, 1755, the Rt. Honourable the Lord Mayor sent out, at six in the morning, from the Mansion House in his Coach and six - attended by the Sword Bearer, the Water Bailiff and the City's Solicitor, for Leigh in Essex, where they arrived about Six in that evening, and lay there that night at one Johnson's at the King's Head. The next morning at Nine a clock The Lord Mayor walk to Crow Stone point; Eastwood of and two miles from Leigh, and in the Parish of Prittlewell, where a hole was dug, within High Water Mark, and a Pillar placed therein of Portland Stone as a Mark of the limits of the City of London's jurisdiction, on the Essex side of the River of Thames, being the exact spot where the Ancient Mark of Pillar of this City's Boundaries was formerly fixt, according to the Memories of the Oldest Men now living in Leigh or the Neighbourhood.

The full length of the Pillar now erected is Six feet six inches and is Four feet four inches above the surface of the ground; Each Square side being of Twenty Inches. On the Square side facing the River are cut in the Stone

The Arms of the City of London 1285

And on the Square side facing the land

God Preserve the City of London

And on a Square Copper Plate wrap up in Lead under the Stone is engraved as follows:

This Stone was replaced by
The Right Honourable STEPHEN THEODORE JANNSSEN Esqr.
Lord Mayor of the City of London and Conservator of the River of Thames
and Waters on the
25th of August &
in the 29th Year of the Reign of His Majesty
King George the Second
NB At this Ceremony there were distributed on the Spot, by the Lord Mayor about
Three Hundred Silver Pennys and Two Pences to Eighty or Ninety Children belonging
to the Parish of Leigh."

This Crowstone was presented in 1950 to the Priory Park Museum, Prittlewell in
Essex, by the Port of London of London Authority. It now stands proudly erect, in
Priory Park, a symbol, of the might and power of the Corporation of the City of
London.

Three sides of this stone bear inscriptions. They are as follows:

NORTH FACE

GOD
PRESERVE
THE CITY OF
LONDON

CHARLES FLOWER ESQR.
LORD MAYOR
1809

MATTHEW WOOD ESQR.
LORD MAYOR
1816

WILLIAM HEYGATE ESQ.
LORD MAYOR
1823

RT. HONOURABLE W THOMPSON
LORD MAYOR
1829

EAST FACE:

BRASS CROSBY
LORD MAYOR
1771

RICHARD CLARKE ESQ.

LORD MAYOR
1785
W W GILL ESQR.
LORD MAYOR
1789

W CURTIS ESQ.
LORD MAYOR
1796

SIR JOHN EAMER KNT.
LORD MAYOR
1802

WEST FACE:

WILLIAM COPELAND
LORD MAYOR
1835

But who were these Lord Mayors? The London Record Office sent biographical notes on these dignitaries. The first name inscribed on the stone was:

SIR CHARLES FLOWER

20th April, 1784. Sir Charles was admitted to the Freedom of the City of London by servitude in the Framework Knitters' Company. Sir Charles Flower worked as a Framework Knitter at Cornhill.

1798 Unsuccessfully contested Aldermanic election for Portsoken Ward.

1799-1800   Sheriff

1801-1802   Master of the Framework Knitters' Company

29th May 1801 - 27th May 1834   Alderman for Cornhill Ward

1808-1809   Lord Mayor

During his Mayoralty the City mounted lavish celebrations to mark the fiftieth anniversary of the accession of George III. On 25th October the Corporation went in procession to St Paul's in the afternoon and to a dinner given by the Lord Mayor at the Mansion House in the evening. The Mansion House was grandly decorated with oak, thistle and shamrock. Merchants and bankers met at Merchant Taylors' Hall, where they were joined by several of the nobility. Many of the chief companies met in their respective halls. The Bank, Mansion House, East India House, Lloyd's Coffee House, the Royal Exchange and the Post Office were all illuminated. Shortly after these celebrations the King created the Lord Mayor a baronet.

1812-1814   Treasurer of the London Hospital.

27th May, 1834   Resigned from the office of Alderman due to ill-health: "The state of my health is such as to warrant my coming to the conclusion that it is not likely I shall be again able to perform the duties of the office with satisfaction to myself, my resignation therefore is clearly incumbent upon me; and as I am now only trespassing on the kindness of my friends I feel that in justice to them I ought not to do so any longer.

15th September 1834 Died and was buried in Aldgate churchyard, leaving a fortune of £555,000 which had been accumulated Government contracts for provisions in time of war.

The second Mayor inscribed was:

MATTHEW WOOD

Born in Tiverton in 1768 and was educated there at Blundell's Free Grammar School. He started his working life as a serge-maker at Tiverton before being apprenticed as a chemist and druggist. He eventually opened up a business independently in Bishops-gate, London, where he came aged twenty-two. Later he became a hop merchant.

His civic career commenced in 1802 when he was elected Common Councilman for Cripplegate Ward. He became Deputy of the same ward in 1806 and was elected Alderman on 14th September 1807, He was Sheriff of London in 1809-10 and Lord Mayor in 1815-16 and again in 1816-17, his re-election to the Mayoralty being a distinction achieved by very few men in modern times. When he was sheriff in 1809 he arrested Francis Burdett, who protested against the suspension of the Habeas Corpus Act and was sent to the Tower for breach of privilege. When he was Lord Mayor he built the City state barge at a cost of £5,000, a considerable sum. He named the barge after his daughter, Maria Wood. The barge was used for many ceremonial visits including one to the City Stone at Staines.

Wood became MP for London in 1817 and remained in Parliament until 1843. He had previously contested elections at London in 1812 and Grampound in 1814. A member of the Fishmongers' Company, he was Prime Warden of that Company from 1834-36, Governor of the Irish Society from 1835-43 and was created a baronet by Queen Victoria at the Guildhall on October 9th, 1837, the first title the Queen bestowed. It was because of Wood that the future Queen Victoria was born on English instead of foreign soil, as he made arrangements for the Duke and Duchess of York to be resident in this country for the birth. His wife was Maria, daughter of John Page, a surgeon of Woodbridge, Suffolk. When he died, on 25th September 1843, he left three sons: John Page Wood who succeeded him in the baronetcy and was the father of Field Marshall Sir Evelyn Wood; William Page Wood, who became Lord Chancellor and was raised to the peerage with the title of Lord Hatherley; and Western Wood who was also MP for the City.

A leader of the advanced Liberal Party in the City, Matthew Wood was perhaps best known for the prominent part that he played in the affairs of the unfortunate Queen Caroline, the wife of George IV. It was in his house in South Audley Street that she first found shelter on her return from abroad. He was Caroline's chief friend and counsellor. His vehement support of the Queen caused him to be the butt of Theodore

Hook who satirised him in *John Bull* as 'Absolute Wisdom'.

"And who were attending her - heigh ma'am, ho ma'am?

Who were attending her, ho?

Lord Hood for a man,

For a maid Lady Anne,

And Alderman Wood for a beau - beau

And Alderman Wood for a beau."

Caroline of Brunswick, 1762-1821 was the wife of King George IV. It was a very unhappy marriage. George tried to divorce her upon ascending the throne in 1820, offering her an annuity of £50,000 on the proviso that she would renounce her title of Queen of England and live abroad. Caroline refused and returned to London where on 19th July, 1821, she was humiliated by banging on the doors of Westminster Abbey during the coronation and being refused admittance. When she later died there were rioting in the streets protesting at her bad treatment.

The third Lord Mayor inscribed on the Crowstone is that of Sir William Heygate, a local man born in Southend. He was the eldest son of Nicholas Heygate who died in 1774. The Heygates can trace their family back to 1557, Thomas Higate, Highate or Heygate, of Hayes, in Middlesex who was Field Marshal General of the Army before St Quintin under the Earl of Pembroke and became Provost Marshal in Scotland in 1560. Sir William Heygate had a distinguished career and was created a baronet by William IV in 1831. His younger son, James Heygate bought and resided in Porters, which is now used as a mayoral residence in Southend. James died on 22nd July, 1873, aged 80, and is buried in the family grave in Prittlewell churchyard.

SIR WILLIAM HEYGATE, BART.

1782	Born in Southend, 17th May
1806	Free by redemption of the City and the Merchant Taylors' Company, June
1809	Unsuccessfully contested aldermanic elections for Cheap Ward
1809-12	Common Councilman for Cripplegate Within
1811-12	Sheriff
1812-43	Alderman for Coleman Street
1818-26	MP for Sudbury, Suffolk
1822-23	Lord Mayor
1843-44	Chamberlain
1844	Died in office, 28th August

The next mayor on the list is Right Honourable William Thompson, 1829, but there are very few details to be found about him.

William Thompson was elected alderman in 1822. He was a wealthy ironmaster of Tredegar, Wales. As Lord Mayor he laid the foundation stone of Southend Pier, the erection of which commenced in 1830.

The next name on the east face of the stone is that of Brass Crosby.

BRASS CROSBY

1725   Born in Stockton-upon-Tees; apprenticed to an attorney in Sunderland.

      Later practised as an attorney in London, first in Little Minories, later in Seething Lane. Married successively three wealthy widows.

1758-65   Common Councilman for Tower ward.

1760-61   Remembrancer, a person who reminds, a recorder. A remembrancer was an officer of exchequer who was responsible for collecting debts that were due to the Crown. The post also meant that he was representative of the City of London to Parliamentary committees (paying £3,600 for the office).

1764-65   Sheriff

1765-93   Alderman for Bread Street ward.

1770-71   Lord Mayor

When Brass Crosby was elected Lord Mayor, he declared that, at the risk of his life, he would protect the just privileges and liberties of the City of London.

Member originally of the Musicians' Company, translated to the Goldsmiths' Company 13th May, 1766, and was Prime Warden of the Goldsmiths, 1767-68. Was also Auditor of the Chamberlain's and Bridgemasters' accounts 1763-65; President of the Honourable Artillery Company 1780-93; Treasurer of Bethlem and Bridewell Hospitals, 1781-82, and President 1782-93; Governor of the Irish Society, 1785-93. Contested London at elections in 1774 and 1784, and was MP for Honiton, 1768-74. Was on Commission of the Peace for Surrey, as well as being JP for the City of London (by virtue of holding office as Alderman). Especially famous for the part played with Alderman John Wilkes and Alderman Richard Oliver in defence of the freedom of the press and the right to publish parliamentary debates. In 1771 (while Lord Mayor) he was committed to the Tower on this account.

It was in February, 1771, the year he visited the Crowstone, that he became involved in his famous struggle against the House of Commons over the publication of parliamentary debates and the freedom of the press. The printer of the *London Evening Post*, Miller, was arrested by the House. This caused an outcry. The printer was released on the orders of Brass Crosby, Richard Oliver and John Wilkes. For this act of defiance, Crosby was ordered to attend the Bar of the House of Commons. This he did, although he was suffering a lot of pain at the time from a severe attack of gout. Crosby was committed to the Tower of London on 2nd March, 1771. There he stayed until Parliament was dissolved the following July, despite great indignation throughout the country at the imprisonment of a free-minded and free-spirited man only incarcerated for his beliefs in the rights of man. Crosby became a public hero and received the thanks of the Common Council.

In 1772 Common Council voted that a silver cup be presented to Crosby "for the noble stand he made in the business of the Printers". The cup and cover were presented to the Mansion House by Lord Wakefield in 1935.

1793   Died on 14th February at Blackfriars and was buried on his estate in Chelsfield, near Orpington, Kent.

Here was a dramatic person actually being committed to the Tower for his beliefs in freedom.   His associate, the colourful character, John Wilkes (1725-1797), has an impressive life story.   An exceedingly ugly man with a squint, Wilkes was also very charismatic.   He used to boast that he had: "a month's start of his rival on account of his face", and that he could secure the affections of any lady that he fancied.   He had a great sense of humour, perhaps best illustrated in his reply to Lord Sandwich's declaration that Wilkes would either die of the pox or the gallows.   To this he gave the inventive and humorous answer: "That depends, my lord, whether I embrace your mistress or your principles."   A vivid and evocative personality, Wilkes was a member of the legendary Hell Fire Club.

John Wilkes started his public campaign for freedom when he founded the political newspaper, the *North Briton* in 1762.   He used the pages of this publication to print a devastating attack on what he called false ministerial statements in the King's speech on 23rd April of the next year.   Ministers were incensed.   A general warrant was issued and 48 people were arrested and Wilkes was thrown into the Tower of London.   This caused a public outcry and he was released a week later on the grounds that his arrests infringed his privileges as an MP as Member for Aylesbury, a post he held after spending £7000 on an election campaign, much of it to bribe voters.   He later won damages against the secretary of state, the Earl of Halifax, for illegal arrest.   When asked by a Frenchman about the existence of freedom of the press in England, replied: "I cannot tell, but I am trying to find out."   Arguments got so heated that Wilkes got wounded in a duel provoked by exchanges in the House.   He was in various angry debates on the rights of man including those in which involved Brass Crosby.

The next Lord Mayor mention on the Crowstone is Richard Clark.

1739   Born 23rd March in St Botolphs without Aldgate, city of London, son of Richard Clark, citizen & joiner, & Mary his wife (who died 2nd March, 1793, and 21st October, 1795, respectively).

Admitted attorney and built up considerable practice.   Legal pupil of Sir John Hawkins by whom he was introduced to Dr. Samuel Johnson, Member of Essex Head Club & Fellow of Society of Antiquaries (elected 1785).   Bought Porch House in Guildford Street, Chertsey, Surrey, in 1774.   Contested London unsuccessfully 1781.

1776   Married Margaret (daughter of John Pistor, woollen-draper of Walthamstow) by whom he had two sons.

1776-98   Alderman for Broad Street ward

1777-78   Sheriff

1784-85   Mayor

1793-1831 Chamberlain of City of London.
          Member of Joiners' Company & Master 1811-12.
          Colonel White's Regiment 1778-89, 3rd London Militia 1789-94.

Treasurer Bethlem & Bridewell 1781-1831; President Christ's Hospital 1785-98.

Police Magistrate Hatton Garden 1792-98.

1831   Died 16th January, buried at Chertsey.

The next Lord Mayor on the list is William Gill.

Elected Alderman of Walbrook Ward on 24th February, 1781, when he defeated Richard Alsager, citizen and clothworker, on a show of hands. Gill was formerly a Common Councilman of the same ward (from 1764).

A liveryman of the Stationers' Company, Gill was Master of the Company in 1780-81.

Sheriff of London & Middlesex, 1781-82

Treasurer of Christ's Hospital, 1785-98, and elected President in 1798.

Lord Mayor of London 1788-89

Died 26th March, 1798, aged 78, at the Treasurer's House of Christ's Hospital.

William was the son of William Gill of Bexley, Kent, but came to London from Maidstone in 1737, having been born in that town. He carried on business as a wholesale stationer in partnership with Alderman Thomas Wright (Lord Mayor 1785-6) first on London Bridge and afterwards in Abchurch Lane.

The next Lord Mayor that of William Curtis who started his career as a relatively humble sugar baker.

Originally a sugar baker at Wapping. His parents traded in ships' biscuits. Become freeman of Drapers' Company by redemption, 31st May, 1785.

c. 1790 established banking firm of Robarts, Curtis, Were, Homyold and Berwick at 35 Cornhill. Moved in 1797 to 15 Lombard Street, becoming by 1805 Robarts, Curtis, Robarts and Curtis and in 1818 Sir William Curtis, Robarts and Curtis. Robarts, Curtis & Co. later amalgamated with Lubbock, Forster & Co. (1860).

1785-1821   Alderman for Tower ward.

1821-29   Alderman for Bridge Without ward.

1788-89   Sheriff.

1795-96   Mayor

1802   December. Created Baronet.

1795-1829 President of Honourable Artillery Company (Vice-President 1793-95, Lieut. Col. 1804-06, Colonel 1806-17).

1800, September. Commanded SE Division of Loyal London Volunteers at time of bread riots in City.

1810-29   Collector of Orphans' Coal Duties.

1813-29   President of Christ's Hospital.

1806-29   Treasurer of London Institution.

It is interesting that William Curtis was involved in controlling the bread riots in the City in September, 1800. The industrial revolution had produced vast social changes. People moved from their rural communities into the towns and cities. This caused major social unrest. Volunteers were called up to control the angry crowds. As a man of stature William Curtis did his duty and commanded one of the volunteer bands organised to bring back order to the City.

He was civic leader of the Tories for many years and favourite subject of satire for Whigs, who favoured industrial and commercial development and were in power continually from 1714-60. When the Reform Bill of 1832 was passed the Whigs became known as the Liberals.

Curtis was badly educated and a poor speaker. But he became a leading Tory and as such a but of Whig jokes. Examples of which are: "The fat knight and the Petition". It was said that; "No man of his time was ever the subject of so much ridicule."

MP for London 1790-1818 and 1820-26; for Bletchingley 1819-20; and for Hastings 1826.

He was a very good friend of George IV. In fact, the King often stayed with Curtis at his house at Ramsgate. He is popularly credited with the origin of that popular phrase 'the three Rs'. He died 18th January, 1826, at Ramsgate and great crowds attended his funeral. Curtis's remains are interred in the crypt of St Mary's, Wanstead Parish Church.

The last name of the east face of the Crowstone is that of Sir John Earner, a very flamboyant man.

According to the *City Biography* (a not entirely reliable source), Sir John "Formerly kept a small grocer's shop in Leadenhall Street ... he now carries on the wholesale grocery business in Wood Street, Cheapside." His widow, Mary, died on 13th August, 1842, aged 83. Earner's daughter, Augusta Caroline, married Nathaniel Kemp of Ovingdean, Sussex, on 27th May, 1823.

1774, June.   Freeman of the City of London by redemption in the Salters' Company
1794-5   Sheriff
1795-1823   Alderman for Langbourn Ward
1795   15th April. Knighted
1796   Contested the parliamentary seat of Ilchester as a Tory
1796-1803   Lt. Colonel West London Militia

1800, 15th September. Played a prominent part in keeping order in the City in the face of bread riots.

1801-2   Mayor. On Lord Mayor's Day the London crowd celebrated the signing of an agreement with the French Republic to settle a definite peace. The Treaty of Amiens was signed on 27th March, 1802. The signatures were France, Britain, Spain, and Holland. It ended the first phase of the bloody and long cut-throat and aggressive French Revolutionary and Napoleonic Wars. The treaty was alas only a truce and the wars resumed in May, 1803.

1803-20   He was Colonel of the East London Militia. In 1806 Earner was acquitted by a General Court Martial on charges preferred against him by Captain William Ayres. The officers, non-commissioned officers and privates of the East London Regiment presented Earner with a sword celebrating his acquittal and the displacement of his accuser and four other officers 'from the Regiment by the express Command of the Sovereign'.

1805 ———— Master of the Salters' Company

1814-23   Police Magistrate for Southwark. In 1821 Earner was unable to fulfil his duty of daily attendance at Southwark Town Hall because he was afflicted 'with serious attacks of apoplexy'.

1823   29th March.   Died, aged seventy three years. Sir John Earner was buried at Ovingdean in Sussex.

Sir John Earner was a colourful character, not unacquainted with controversy. On 29th July, 1806, Earner was prosecuted for assault and false imprisonment at the Maidstone assizes by James Parnell, an higgler (a peddler). The case arose after Eamer's curricle (a two-wheeled open chaise, drawn by two horses abreast), collided with Parnell's horse cart. There was an altercation during which Earner struck Parnell about the head with a horse whip. The jury found for the plaintiff, who was awarded £10 and costs.

On a lighter note, Welch records in *The Modern History of the City of London*, 1896, the following event:

'An amusing hoax played on Alderman Sir John Earner resulted in a considerable number of persons calling at his house, under the impression that they were invited to dinner. The worthy Alderman made the best of the situation and his guests spent an hilarious evening'. It is this hoax that Sir John Earner is best remembered.

There is only one name inscribed on the west face of the Crowstone, that of William Copeland.

Born 24th March, 1797, only son of William Copeland of Stoke on Trent and London, merchant and pottery manufacturer and his wife, Mary, née Fowler. He was the son of the partner of Josiah Spode the porcelain manufacturer.

Member of the Goldsmiths' Company: elected to the Livery, 20th January, 1824, elected to the Court of Assistants 24th October 1828, Prime Warden of the Company, 1837-8 and 1851-2.

Freedom of the City of London by redemption June, 1820.

Married 29th April, 1826, Sarah, daughter of John Yates of Shelton, Staffordshire: she died 22nd March, 1860. They had eight sons and two daughters - those who survived their father were: William Fowler Mountford, born 4th November, 1828; Edward Capper, born 28th November, 1835; Alfred James, born 6th April, 1837; Richard Pine, born 27th September, 1841.

He was a pottery manufacturer, partner in and, from 1st March, 1833, proprietor, at first with Thomas Garrett, of the Spode china business (established by Josiah Spode, 1770, later known as Copeland and Garrett, subsequently as W T Copeland and Sons). As a manufacturer of porcelain productions, especially those of Parian groups and statuettes, he gained world wide renown.

Alderman of Bishopsgate, 1829-68, Sheriff, 1828-9, Lord Mayor, 1835-6. President of Bethlem and Bridewell Hospitals, 1861-8, and of the Honourable Artillery Company,

1854-68.

MP for Coleraine, 1831-2, 1833-7, and Stoke-on-Trent, 1837-52 and 1857-65. Contested Stoke-on-Trent unsuccessfully, 1852.

William Taylor Copeland died 12th April, 1868, at Russell Farm (Russells), Watford, Hertfordshire. Buried at Watford Cemetery 18th April, 1868.

THE TALLER STONE

The taller and newer stone that was situated in the Thames was erected in 1838. This is shaped like Cleopatra's Needle on the Embankment. This also has names and dates inscribed in its flank:

WEST FACE

> RIGHT HON. WILLIAM
> TAYLOR COPELAND
> LORD MAYOR
> JOHN LAWSON ESQ. ALD.
> DAVID SALOMONS ESQ.
> SHERIFFS
>
> GOD
> PRESERVE THE CITY OF
> LONDON
> 1836

SOUTH FACE

> 1842
> SIR JOHN PIRIE BART.
> 1849
> SIR JAMES DUKE
> 1856
> DAVID SALOMONS ESQRE.

EAST FACE

> SIR WILLIAM HEYGATE BART.
> WILLIAM VENABLES ESQURE.
> JAMES WHITE ESQ.
> ALDERMEN
> JAMES DUKE ESQ.
> JOHN JOHNSON ESQ.
> SHERIFFS ELECT
> WALTER ANDERSON PEACOCK
> JONATHAN CHARLES PRIOR
> JOSEPH THOMPSON

COMMON COUNCIL
ROBERT FINCH NEWMAN
SOLICITOR
NATHAN SAUNDERS
WATER BAILIFF
SAMUEL BEDDOWE
COMMON CRYER
JAMES FRANCIS FIRTH
TOWN CLERK

When the smaller Crowstone was removed to Priory Park in 1950, the Port of London Authority had a plaque attached to the newer and taller stone to mark its absence. On this was inscribed:

"This boundary stone, known as the Crowstone, was erected in 1837 to mark the seaward limit at that time of the city of London's jurisdiction over the River Thames. Beside it stood a smaller stone erected by the Lord Mayor of London on 25th August 1755, which was removed to Priory Park, Southend-on-Sea in the year 1950."

The names on the east face of the stone represent those officials who accompanied the Lord Mayor, David Salomons, on the last ceremonial visit to the Crowstone in 1856. After this date the jurisdiction of the river was passed from the City of London to the Thames Conservancy.

Of the Lord Mayors themselves. William Taylor Copeland appeared on the West face of the smaller Crowstone and I have given the details accordingly. The next name on the list, John Lawson, I cannot find any case history.

But here is the profile of the remarkable Sir David Salomons. He was the City's first Jewish Alderman: a considerable feat, as at that time there was still substantial anti-Semitism in public life:

Born 22nd November, 1797, second son of Levy Salomons, a Jewish merchant and underwriter of London and Frant, Sussex, and Matilda de Metz/Mitz of Leyden. The family had long been resident in London, in commerce.

1832 became one of the founders of the London and Westminster Bank. When he died, he was its last surviving governor.

1834, commenced business as an underwriter.

David Salomons was a liveryman of the Coopers Company. He made many donations to charities. It was in recognition of his vast contributions to good causes that he was chosen as sheriff of London and Middlesex in 1835. This was a vast honour, for he was the first Jewish sheriff. In fact up to this time no person of the Jewish faith could be admitted to any municipal office.

In 1835 he was elected as an Alderman for Aldgate. He being Jewish also caused problems. The Court of Alderman protested at the validity of his election. But Salomons won his case, although the verdict was reversed on appeal to the High Court.

1849, admitted a member of the Middle Temple.

The City's first Jewish Alderman, Sheriff and Lord Mayor. On his election as Sheriff, a special Act was passed to set at rest any legal doubts over his election. He was twice elected Alderman, but was unable to serve due to refusing to take the Christian oath of office. In 1845 an Act was passed allowing Jews to hold municipal offices largely due to Salomons exertions, and so he could take office when elected Alderman of Cordwainer in 1847. As a celebration, he founded a £50 annual prize at the City of London School.

Alderman, Aldgate, elected 19th November, 1835 [did not serve].

Alderman, Portsoken elected 27th September, 1844 [did not serve].

Alderman, Cordwainer, elected 6th December, sworn 14th December, 1847-18th July, 1873. Sheriff, 1835-1836.

Lord Mayor, 1855-1856. As a character reference to acknowledge his work on bringing about religious freedom, a testimonial was presented to by his co-religionists. This stated: "an acknowledgement of his exertions in the cause of religious liberty."

Free of the Coopers' Company 5th July, 1831: Master, 1841-1842.

Free of the City of London by redemption through the Coopers' Company, May 1832.

Baronet of Broomhill, Tunbridge, Kent, created October, 1869

Sheriff of Kent, 1839-1840.

1st Jewish magistrate of Kent, appointed 1838.

Magistrate and Deputy Lieutenant of Kent, Sussex & Middlesex.

Contested Shoreham, 1837; Maidstone, 1841; Greenwich, 1847, 1852

MP for Greenwich 1851-1852, 1859-1873 (Liberal)

When first elected MP, refused to take Christian oath but spoke and voted anyway, for which he was fined £500. He was judged to have great experience in Parliament on commercial and financial questions.

Married (1) on 18th April, 1825, Jeannette, daughter of Solomon Cohen of Grove House, Canonbury, Middlesex. She died in March 1867.

(2) on 23rd September, 1872, Cecilia, widow of P. J. Salomons esq. of Upper Wimpole Street.

No issue, but by special provision, his heir to the baronetcy was his nephew, David Lionel Salomons, (born 1851), only son of his brother Peter.

Died at his house in Great Cumberland Place, Hyde Park on 18th July, 1873.

Buried at the Jew's Cemetery, West Ham, Essex.

Left a legacy of £1,000 to the Guildhall Library, partly used to augment the collection of Hebrew and Jewish works presented by his brother Philip, and partly to purchase books on commerce and art.

On the south face of the taller Crowstone is

SIR JOHN PIRIE, BART.

Born on 18th September, 1781, the eldest son of John Pirie of Duns, Berwickshire.

By 1807 he was engaged in the business of a merchant ship broker and ship owner of No. 5. Pope's Head Alley, London. He was one of the Peninsular and Oriental Steam Navigation Company's original directors on the incorporation of the company in 1840.

He held the post of Deputy Chairman of the company from 1848 until his death.

1828-29 Liveryman and Master of the Plaisterers' Company

1831-32 Sheriff

1834-51 Alderman for Cornhill Ward

1841 Contested the Parliamentary election for London

1841-42 Lord Mayor. Created baronet on 13th April, 1842, in consequence of the birth of the Prince of Wales during his mayoralty

1842-51 President of St Thomas' Hospital

1843 Stood as candidate for the office of City Chamberlain

1851 27th February Died, aged seventy, at Champion Hill, Camberwell.

The next name on the side of the taller Crowstone is -

Sir James Duke, who was a liveryman of the Spectacle Makers' Company. He was elected sheriff in 1836 and alderman in 1840. He was knighted in 1837 and became MP for Boston, Lincolnshire. From 1837-41 Sir James Duke was created a baronet in 1849. He was elected MP for the City of London in 1849, the post having been vacant for six years.

He left a graphic account of the ceremonies at the Crowstone which was published in the *Illustrated London News* and later in the *Southend Standard*.

The last name on the south face of the Crowstone is that of David Salomons who life I have already described.

THE CEREMONIAL VISITS

The Lord Mayor of London visited the Crowstone once every seven years. These engagements were a time of great ceremony. Elaborate rituals were held and there was much pageantry. It was a colourful occasion. There were thirteen of these majestic ceremonial observances, the first being in 1771 and the last in 1856, after which the Thames came under the control of the Thames Conservancy Board.

The City of London took their duties about the care of the Thames seriously. They held eight Courts of Conservancy annually. At each of these sessions enquiries were made concerning misuses of the river, whether illegal weirs or kiddells had been erected or fish destroyed. The courts were presided by the Lord Mayor, Aldermen, Sheriffs and Officers of the City of London and were held at Southwark, Greenwich, and Stratford. After the proceedings there would be a fine dinner.

Surveys were also made to check the western boundaries with a formal visit to the City Stone at Staines every seventh year. Similar visits were made to check the limits on the eastern confines of the City's jurisdiction on the Thames and Medway. During these trips a paddle steamer was chartered and the Lord Mayor's party would travel from Greenwich to Chalkwell and later to Upnor on the Medway. Before Southend Pier was erected in 1830, the Lord Mayor, the Water Bailiff, Sheriffs and Aldermen of the City of London would land in Southend in small boats. This was a time of gaiety and pageantry. Some of the visitors remained on board the paddle steamer, while the Lord Mayor stayed in the prestigious Royal Hotel. At this eminent hotel, a rich dinner was consumed followed by dancing. The people of the town were not forgotten on this top-ranking and unforgettable occasion, there was a magnificent display of fireworks on the cliffs.

The next afternoon, the Lord Mayor's party and local dignitaries drove in carriages along the cliffs to the Crowstone. Here massed crowds awaited them, all eager to view the spectacle. Depending on the state of the tide the Crowstone was reached either by foot or small boats. Banners of the City of London were held by people mounting the smaller stone and after 1836, the taller one. Now the City Sword was placed against the stone, this symbolised the official maintenance of the City of London of the River Thames. When this ritual occurred at high tide, the conservators rowed round the Crowstone three times and then were served wine and drank the toast: "God preserve the City of London". At low tide an enthralling ceremony occurred. Sheriffs wishing for the honour of Freedom of the Water were "respectfully bumped" on the stone local waterman. The waterman paid two guineas to participate in the ritual which called "bumping" or "immunity". Finally to the further enjoyment of the crowds the proceedings concluded with a scramble in the mud for coins thrown to the crowd by the Lord Mayor. Usually one hundred newly minted sixpences were dispersed in this manner.

This must have been a very glittering and showy event. The local historian Benton described it as a "gorgeous water pageants". It was like a Lord Mayor's show of the river.

To mark the occasion the Lord Mayor's name was inscribed on to the Crowstone together with the date of the ritual. The party then returned to the Royal Hotel and then back to the steamer which then sailed up the Medway to Rochester. Here they were received by the Mayor of Rochester. A similar ceremony followed at the London Stone, on the bank of the Medway at Upnor, and again the party enjoyed an evening of feasting and dancing. The next day, the festivities over, the party returned to Greenwich.

There is a wonderful description of this fascinating ritual in the *Morning Chronicle* of August 3rd ,1816. It is very detailed and conjures up an evocative and fun filled event. The piece is entitled "The Septennial View of the Boundaries of the Jurisdiction of City of London in the Rivers Thames and Medway."

It is reproduced in full:

"Last week the Lord Mayor took a view of the boundaries of the jurisdiction of the city of London, in the rivers Thames and Medway, which takes place once in seven years. His Lordship embarked on board the Trinity yacht, at Blackwall, on Tuesday morning, the 23rd with the Lady Mayoress, and several other ladies, the Aldermen and City Officers, and several persons of distinction who had been invited on the occasion, and under a salute of guns immediately set sail, accompanied by a number of other yachts and vessels, amongst which were the Honourable East India Company's yacht, the beautiful fast sailing yacht belonging to the Marquis of Anglesea, having on board the Marquis and Marchioness, the ladies Paget and Lord Erskine; the Wellington packet, with a select Committee of the Common Council of the City of London; and the Jubilee, with the excellent band of music belonging to his Royal Highness the Duke of Kent, who had handsomely ordered them to attend the Lord Mayor during the whole of his voyage. In Erith Reach his Lordship was met, and joined by Admiral Sir Charles Rowley and his family, in his yacht, and by the Honourable Courtenay Boyle, Commissioner of Sheerness, in his yacht, with his family and Sir George and Lady Hoste, who severally came on board the Trinity yacht, to pay their respects to the Lord Mayor, and partook of the refreshments which were provided.

Off Gravesend the Lord Mayor was joined by the Earl and Countess of Darnley and Lord Clifton. His Lordship arrived off Southend about five in the afternoon, and having cast anchor, the company sat down to an elegant cold dinner on board the Trinity yacht. Soon after dinner the Company went on shore in the Water Bailiff's eight oared shallop [a light open boat], and the different row-boats which had attended his Lordship, to prepare themselves for the ball given by the Lord Mayor and Lady Mayoress, at the Royal Hotel, and notwithstanding the tide was much out, and the great distance the yacht were obliged to anchor, every one got comfortably and safe on shore.

The Marquis of Anglesea and the party in his yacht left the Lord Mayor when they arrived off Southend, and returned to London. The ball at the Royal Hotel at Southend was numerously and elegantly attended, and was as splendid as had ever been witnessed at that place: and the supper to which upwards of two hundred persons sat down, by the judicious arrangements which his Lordship had previously made, and the exertions of the Master of the Hotel would have done credit to the first Taverns in London. During the evening a brilliant display of fireworks, under the direction of Mrs. Hengler, who is employed at Vauxhall, took place at the terrace, in front of the assembly room windows. The dancing which recommenced after supper did not cease until near five o'clock in the morning. The Lord Mayor and the Lady Mayoress did not enter the ball-room until after ten o'clock, in consequence of one of his Lordship's packages, which held his clothes, through some neglect, not having been brought on shore, and the time it occupied to get it after it was missed.

On the following morning, Wednesday, the 25th, the Lord Mayor and his party proceeded in carriages to Crowstone Point, below Leigh, where the city stone is placed, which marks the extent of the jurisdiction eastward in the river Thames, on the Essex shore, and a mason being in waiting, immediately cut upon the stone the Lord Mayor's name, with the date of the year; and his Lordship then placed the state sword against the stone, and claimed the city's jurisdiction to that part of the river, after which his Lordship and the company with him drank "God preserve the City of London."

In consequence of the spring tide, the whole of the foregoing ceremony was performed in boats; and when his Lordship returned to the shore, he distributed amongst the people assembled pieces of new silver coin and wine.

On their return to Southend the company embarked on board the different yachts, and sailed for the Medway; and on passing Sheerness his Lordship was saluted and cheered from the shore, and was also saluted by the Admiral's and other ships lying there, which were returned from the Trinity Yacht and the vessels in his Lordship's company. Soon after passing Sheerness his Lordship was met by numerous vessels and boats with their colours flying, filled with the Members of the Corporation of Rochester, and company from that place, Chatham and Stroud, and attended by several bands of music. The Mayor and Corporation of Rochester having that day held their Admiralty Court for the opening of the oyster beds; the vessels and boats were more numerous than upon any former occasion, and added very considerably to the splendour of the scene. The wind and tide not permitting the Trinity Yacht in which the Lord Mayor's company was, to reach Rochester before dark, they were divided and carried to Rochester by the boats attending his Lordship, and several that were politely offered belonging to the vessels that came down to meet him.

When the company arrived at the Crown Inn, Rochester, they found every accommodation provided for them by Mr. Wright, the master of the house.

On the next morning, Thursday, the 26th, it having been too late the preceding night, when the Lord Mayor arrived, the Mayor and Corporation of Rochester were severally introduced to his Lordship at the Crown Inn, and then retired to their Town Hall.

Soon after breakfast his Royal Highness the Duke of Sussex arrived from town and joined his Lordship's company when preparations were immediately made for the procession to take water to proceed to the City Stone by Upnor Castle, which marks the boundary of the Lord Mayor's jurisdiction at the Medway. As soon as his Lordship's procession was formed in the Crown Inn yard, they were joined by the Mayor and Corporation of Rochester its full regalia, with all their Officers attending them. The company then proceeded to the water side, his Royal Highness the Duke of Kent's band, the Lord Mayor's and Sheriff's servants in their state liveries, and the City's colours, with the banner and Royal Standard going first.

The Mayor and Corporation of Rochester formed on the right of the Lord Mayor, Aldermen and City Officers. His Royal Highness the Duke of Sussex walked between the Lord Mayor and the Mayor of Rochester and the state sword of the City with the point downwards, before the Lord Mayor, who wore his gold collar of SS and the jewel of the City. After taking water several guns were fired from the shore, and a salute was returned from the Trinity yacht and the vessels in the River, when the Mayor and Corporation of Rochester in their yacht, and the Lord Mayor and his company in the Trinity yacht, attended by numerous vessels and boats, proceeded down the river to Upnor Castle, and at the City Stone, the point of the state sword carried before the Lord Mayor being elevated, his Lordship having arrived within his own jurisdiction, the same ceremony of placing the sword, drinking "God preserve the City of London," and claiming the jurisdiction, took place, in the presence of the Mayor and Corporation of Rochester, as at the stone on the Essex shore below Leigh, after which his Lordship distributed wine and new silver coin amongst the populace. The tide not permitting the yachts and sailing vessels to return to Rochester, almost the whole of the company returned in row boats and formed a complete regatta. On the Lord Mayor's arrival at the Crown Inn, the Noblemen and Gentlemen who had been invited to dinner to meet the Corporation of Rochester, were waiting to receive his Lordship, and were severally introduced: and soon after partook of a most sumptuous dinner, at which the Lord and Lady Mayoress presided, having the Mayor of Rochester on his Lordship's right hand.

Amongst the company present were his Royal Highness the Duke of Sussex, the Earl and Countess of Darnley, Lord Clifton, Sir Charles Rowley, Sir Robert Barlow, the Hon. Courtenay Boyle, Sir John Brown, Sir George Hoste, Sir John Louis, Sir James Gordon, Major General Winter, Colonels D'Arcy and Clifford, Mr. Calcraft and Mr. Barnett, the Members for Rochester, several of the Aldermen of London, the principal Officers at Chatham, Maidstone and Sheerness, and almost the whole of the Corporation of Rochester; many other noblemen and gentlemen were invited, but could not attend.

About nine o'clock the company broke up, and were conveyed in carriages provided for the purpose to the Ball given by the Lord Mayor and the Lady Mayoress at the Assembly Rooms which were splendidly fitted up for the occasion with an illumination in the front, composed of variegated lamps, forming the royal crown, with the initial letters of London and Rochester united underneath, the whole encircled by laurel wreaths of green lamps.

The ball was very numerously attended, the Ladies were most elegantly dressed in compliment to the Lady Mayoress, and the display was as brilliant as had ever been witnessed in that city, or in the county of Kent. Besides the Lord Mayor's company most of the respectable families in Chatham and the neighbourhood, with the respective families of the Members of the Corporation of Rochester and the principal inhabitants, and the Naval and Military Officers in the Medway, at Chatham, and the depôt at Maidstone, were present.

Tea, coffee and every refreshment, with ices and fruits that could be required, were most amply provided, and the dancing, which was commenced almost after the Lord and Lady Mayoress with his Royal Highness the Duke of Sussex entered, and was kept up with great spirit, and did not cease until three in the morning, when the company departed much gratified with the entertainment. In the course of the evening a most brilliant display of fireworks was exhibited, under the same direction as at Southend. His Royal Highness the Duke of Sussex accompanied the Earl and Countess of Darnley to Cobham Hall to sleep, and the Lord Mayor and his company from London were accommodated at the Crown Inn.

On Friday morning early, agreeably to a previous invitation from the Earl and Countess of Darnley, who handsomely presented part of the venison at the dinner at the Crown Inn on the preceding day, the Lord Mayor and Lady Mayoress, with the Ladies and Gentlemen in their party, went to Cobham Hall to a public breakfast. After being shown into the grand musical saloon, and introduced to the Earl and Countess of Darnley and their family, the company were ushered into the superb Picture Gallery of Cobham Hall, where the table was spread with every delicacy of the season in great abundance, at which upwards of one hundred persons sat down and experienced the most polite attention from the noble host and hostess. The company consisted chiefly, besides his Royal Highness the Duke of Sussex and the Lord Mayor's and the Lady Mayoress's party, of the principle families in the neighbourhood and many of the ladies, Naval and. Military Officers and Gentlemen who were at the ball at Rochester the preceding evening.

After the company had partaken of the breakfast they perambulated the beautiful grounds surrounding Cobham Hall, his Royal Highness the Duke of Kent's band performing pieces of music the whole time, and on their different carriages being announced, his Royal Highness the Duke of Sussex and the Lord Mayor and Lady Mayoress with his party returned to London highly pleased with the urbanity and attention which had been paid them by the Earl and Countess of Darnley.

The yachts and vessels which accompanied the Lord Mayor to Rochester, sailed on Friday afternoon with such parts of his Lordship's company as preferred returning by water.

There is an equally colourful, thrilling, and exciting description of the remarkable pageant which was printed in the *Southend Standard* in February, 1927. The paper reprints an article which appeared in *The Illustrated London News* of July 12th, 1849, describing the spectacle of this tableau in the town 1849. Again I transcribe the article in full:

LONDON'S LORD MAYOR AT LEIGH.

CONSERVANCY VISIT IN 1849

WHEN COIN SCRAMBLE WAS "ROMUSTRIOUS"

"This celebration in 1849 - the previous one was in 1842, when Sir John Pirie filled the civic chair - according to *The Illustrated London News*, contributed to the convivial memorabilia of the present Mayoralty."

The periodical in question goes on to describe the origin of the custom thus:-

The jurisdiction appears to have been immemorially exercised over both the fisheries and navigation of a large portion of the Thames by the Mayor and Corporation of London, and we find an order dated 1405, issued from Sir John Woodcock, then Lord Mayor, enjoining the destruction of weirs and nets from Staines to the Medway in consequence of the injury which they did to the fishery and their obstruction to the navigation. The portion of the river over which the jurisdiction extended seems to been always much the same. "The offices of Meter and Conservator are asserted from Staines to the mouth of the Thames, the commencement of the city's jurisdiction being marked by a stone with an apocryphal date, called London Stone, placed on the north bank of the river a short distance above the present bridge of Staines; and its termination on the south shore by the formerly navigable creek of Yantlet, separating the Isle of Grain from the mainland of Kent; and on the north shore by the village of Leigh, in Essex, placed directly opposite and close to the lower extremity of Canvey Island." The "View" we are about to describe consisted of visits to the boundary stones at Leigh and Cookham Wood and which took place on the 12th, 13th and 14th inst. [July, 1849].

Then follows the story

The company assembled on board the *Meteor* steamer engaged for the occasion, moored off Brunswick Wharf, Blackwall. There were present the Lord Mayor and Lady Mayoress and a large party.

Captain Rowland attended the View as principal harbour master.

The steamer left Blackwall at about half past eleven o'clock; and, having received on board the Royal Marine band at Woolwich, the *Meteor* proceeded on her passage to Southend, the Civic party being liberally welcomed with salutes and other respectful demonstrations.

At Greenhithe Pier the *Meteor* received on board Mr. James Harmer, from whose delightful seat, Ingress Abbey, a salute was fired.

At about three o'clock, the *Meteor*... arrived at Southend pier, where the Lord Mayor, Lady Mayoress, and a large portion of the company landed. The Lord Mayor, attended by the Aldermen; Mr. Firth, the Town Clerk Mr. Sewell, Clerk of the Chamber; and some of the civic authorities, proceeded in carriages towards Leigh, nearly opposite to which the boundary stone is situated. Here, by direction of his Lordship, the City colours and state sword were placed upon the stone; and, after asserting his rights as Conservator of the River Thames on behalf of the City of London, by prescription and usage from time immemorial, the Lord Mayor directed the Water Bailiff, as sub-conservator, to cause his name and the date of his visit to be inscribed on the boundary stone.

The Lord Mayor then drank, "God preserve the City of London," the inscription on the ancient stone, and, after distributing coin and wine to the spectators, the civic party returned to the steamer... The stone itself was in the water, so that it had to be reached in boats. The scramble for the money was a robustious affair.

During the absence of the Lord Mayor, a large party of the company who had remained on board the steamer partook of a dinner, served up in excellent style by Mr. King. At this dinner Ald. Sir John Key and Sir Chapman Marshall presided.

On the steamer leaving Southend pier, the Lord Mayor was saluted with loud cheers and the *Meteor* proceeded across to Sheerness and up the Medway.

Evidently the partylike atmosphere continued on the steamer, *The Illustrated London News* continues the tale:

"Shortly after, his Lordship, and the rest of the party which had landed at Southend, sat down to dinner, served in the usual style (presumably the very opulent one). The arrangements were admirably carried out, and a very large party supplied with all the delicacies of the season, from the resources on board a steamer of not very large dimensions.

The passage up the Medway was truly delightful; and on approaching Chatham the crew of one of Her Majesty's ships manned the rigging, and loudly cheered the steamer. The dockyard launches were also out on duty, and the crews, poising the oars, hailed the arrival of his lordship with cheers, which were as warmly responded to by the company on the streamer. the bank playing "God save the Queen," and "Rule Britannia," "Hearts of Oak," and "The British Grenadiers".

Dancing was introduced on board the steamer with much spirit.

About eight o'clock the *Meteor* reached Rochester, and the Lord Mayor and Lady Mayoress landed in his lordship's launch. At the steps the Mayor and Corporation of the ancient city of Rochester, accompanied by the Recorder, James Espinasse, Esq. met the Lord Mayor and Lady Mayoress, and offered them a hearty welcome."

A similar ceremony and spectacular pageant was held at Rochester as was previously carried out at Southend.

Ceremony at the Crowstone, 12th July, 1849

BIBLIOGRAPHY

Addison, William - Essex Worthies

Avenue Baptist Church, Southend - Jubilee 1876 - June 1926

Benton, Philip - History of Rochford Hundred, 1886

Birch, Walter De Grey - The Historical Charters & Constitutional Documents of the City of London, 1887

Burrows, John William - Southend on Sea and District Historical Notes, 1909

Burrows, John William - The Development of Southend-on-Sea, 1930

Butler, Lionel & Given-Wilson, Chris - Mediæval Monasteries of Great Britain

Crancher, Steve - Uncle Fred's History of Westcliff

Christy, Miller, *and* Thresh, May - A History of the Mineral Waters and Medicinal Springs of the County of Essex, 1910

Day, James Wentworth - Coastal Adventure

Farmer, David Hugh - The Oxford Dictionary of Saints

Farries, Kenneth G - Essex Windmills

Glennie, Donald - Our Town

Helliwell, Leonard - South East Essex in the Saxon Period

Hill, *Canon* D. Ingram - Canterbury Cathedral

Kelly's Directories

Kenyon, J P - Dictionary of British History

Littlewood, Mr. - My Grandfather's Shop

Morant, Philip - History and Antiquities of Essex, 1768

Payne, Jessie K - Southend-on-Sea: a pictorial history

Pitt-Stanley, Sheila - Legends of Leigh

Pollitt, William - A History of Prittlewell

Pollitt, William - The Rise of Southend

Pollitt, William - Some Literary Associations of Southend on Sea

Reaney, P H - Place Names of Essex, 1935

Sorrel, Mark - The Peculiar People

Southend Waterworks Company - Safeguarding Your Water Supply: the story of Southend Waterworks Company, 1952

St Georges Presbyterian Jubilee 1948 - Handbook

Standard Guide to Southend on Sea, 1931, 1964

Wright, A C - South East Essex in the Danish and Norman Periods

Wright, J R C - Henry of Eastry, Prior of Christchurch, Canterbury, 1285/6-1331: Some materials for his life

Wyatt, W B - The Crowstone at Leigh-on-Sea considered in Relation to other Thames Mark Stones

CONTEMPORARY INFORMATION

The Anglo Saxon Chronicles

Comptus of 1299

Domesday Book

Extent of the Manor of Milton 1309

Indenture - September 14th, 1327

Southend on Sea and District Antiquarian and Historical Society, 1924,1932

Southend-on-Sea Antiquarian and Historical Society Vol. III, No. 1, 1935

PRESS REPORTS

CHELMSFORD CHRONICLE; 15th September, 1797
ESSEX CHRONICLE
EVENING ECHO; 14th October, 1970
ILLUSTRATED LONDON NEWS; July 21st, 1849
PORT OF LONDON AUTHORITY MONTHLY; January-December, 1951: August, 1965,
SOUTHEND AND WESTCLIFF GRAPHIC, SPECIAL ZEPPELIN SUPPLEMENT: 11th May, 1915
SOUTHEND NEWS; 10th May, 1967
SOUTHEND OBSERVER; 14th April, 1943
SOUTHEND PICTORIAL; 4th February, 1950: 12th January, 1953
SOUTHEND STANDARD; 13th August, 1875: July, 1880: 13th March, 1881: 11th April, 1884: 4th
January, 1934: 12th April, 1934: 2nd August, 1934: 25tb & 30th November, 1939: 2nd December, 1939:
1st April, 1943: 28th October, 1964: 20th January, 1965: 9th May, 1966: 23rd June, 1966: 3rd October,
1969: 12th February, 1970: 7th May, 1970: 4th, 18th & 25th June, 1970: 3rd &17th September, 1970:
29th June, 1972: 7th Sept 1972: 23rd January, 1974
SOUTHEND STAR; 27th October, 1964
SOUTHEND TIMES; 30th November, 1928
TIMES REMEMBERED; 28th June, 1973

ACKNOWLEDGEMENTS

I would like to thank Mrs Janet Bull of the Milton Conservation Society without whose help and encouragement this book would not have been written and Miss Caroline White and Ashley Hitchcox for their valuable help.

Thanks also the staff of the Essex Record Office and the Local Studies Department of Southend Central Library, Mr K Crowe of Southend Central Museum for his kind assistance. Lyne Tate of the Lyne Tate Gallery for her many postcards, Mrs D Fisher for the photographs and information of her family, Sister Hilary of Nazareth House for her information, Mr Rayner for his help and antique map, Mr Peter King and Mr Alan Crow for their material about Avenue Road Baptist Church and St Georges Church. I have also to thank Mr Tidder, Mr Dougherty, Miss Barrows, Mr Tom Castleton, Mrs Wicks, Mrs Barradell, Mr Newton, Mr Littlewood, Mrs Keen, for giving me such a picture of the area when they were young.

I would like to record thanks to James R Sewell, the City Archivist for the Corporation of London Records Office, Guildhall, for his assistance in finding various documents concerning the Crowstone and finally I must also thank R R Aspinall, of the Port of London Authority and Museum in Docklands Project, the Museum of London.

Widening Western Esplanade,
20th March, 1911 (*reproduced by
permission of the Essex Record Office*)